I0069857

KHOA-KIM

THE TOP SECRETS THAT SUCCESSFUL REAL ESTATE INVESTORS DON'T TELL YOU

© 2014 KHOA-KIM. ALL RIGHTS RESERVED

ALL RIGHTS RESERVED. NO PART OF THIS WORK MAY BE REPRODUCED OR STORED IN AN INFORMATIONAL RETRIEVAL SYSTEM, WITHOUT THE EXPRESS PERMISSION OF THE PUBLISHER IN WRITING.

ISBN: 978-1-928155-67-6

PUBLISHED BY:
10-10-10 PUBLISHING
MARKHAM, ON
CANADA

Contents

Acknowledgments   v

About the Author   vii

Foreword   ix

Part I: Six Steps to Become a Successful Investor   **1**

Chapter 1: Start from Scratch   3
Chapter 2: Why Real Estate Investment Makes It Easy
to Become a Millionaire   11
Chapter 3: Six Steps to Become a Successful Real Estate
Investor   23

**Part II: Secrets of Investors Who Have Become
Millionaires**   **31**

Chapter 4: Six Thinking Habits of Successful Investors   33
Chapter 5: Strategies to Successful Investments from
Professional Investors   59
Chapter 6: Complete Understanding of the Cycle of the
Economy to Ensure Success   77

Part III: Building an Empire from Scratch   **89**

Chapter 7: Ways to Build an Empire Without Having
Any Money   91
Chapter 8: Ways to Earn Money in Real Estate
Investments   109
Chapter 9: Real Estate Investment Resources for
Investors   127

Chapter 10: Four Ways to Purchase Properties
for a Good Price   135

**Part IV: Rapidly and Steadily Increase Investment
Profits**   **147**

Chapter 11: Ways to Increase the Value of Real
Estate Investments   149
Chapter 12: Principles That Can Ensure Your Success
in Investment   163
Chapter 13: Attract Good Fortune   171

Epilogue   203

Acknowledgments

First and foremost, we would like to thank our parents on both sides of the family: Nhuong Le (Father), Ngoc Bao (Mother) – Loc Do (Mother), Linh Nguyen (Father), and our younger siblings who have unconditionally supported us throughout these years.

We would also like to thank our four children: Thaison, Crystal, Johnny, and Dylan, for bringing us joy and being a great source of motivation for us.

In addition, we are very grateful to our Masters: Master Thich Thong Dat and Hungkar Dorje Rinpoche who have helped and supported us spiritually through the difficult times of our lives.

Thank you Brian Tracy, Robert Kiyosaki, and Donald Trump for teaching us the priceless strategies to become successful and wealthy.

Thank you to the professionals at Peak Potential, especially lecturer T. Harv Eker and Adam Markel, for helping us in realizing our true potentials.

Thank you to all members at Akimax Inc., as well as all members at Reiinvest, Inc., all our collaborators who have worked tirelessly to form a fabulous company.

Thank you Uncle Song Nhi, the director, the editor-in-chief of Nguon magazine, and Ngoc Tran Le for your selflessness in helping with the book.

Thank you to our English teacher, Lisa Rose, for editing and teaching us to use language in a dramatic and effective way, helping our ideas in the book be more fluent.

We also would like to thank our staff and secretary: Anna Pham, Nhu Ho, Nguyen Tran, Kim Phuong Ngo, and Sophia Nguyen, for helping us with the workload even on the weekends and working late into the night so that we would have enough time to complete this book.

About the Author: KhoaKim

KhoaKim is a combined name of the married couple of Khoa Le and Kim Nguyen. They are known as professional real estate investors, who have invested, bought, sold, and managed over 3000 properties in various states such as: Arizona, Nevada, Florida, and in their home state of California over the past 15 years.

Khoa and Kim are also successful business professionals, who have created and founded many companies dealing with buying and selling of real estate, construction, development, and management of properties and financial aspects in various regions of the United States. In addition, they are also looking to expand their business in the Philippines and Vietnam.

Moreover, they are co-authors of the book about investing in real estate called "Maximizing Real Estate Profits Through Trustee Sales and Foreclosures".

Besides investing in real estate and establishing several successful companies, Khoa and Kim also fully dedicate themselves to charities in their free time. They help in raising money for various non-profit organizations that assist homeless people, and build and expand temples, including Sacred Heart Community Service, City team, and Chua Dai Nhat Nhu Lai (Maha Vairocana Temple).

Even with their hectic schedules, Khoa and Kim are also on the board of directors for the non-profit organization of Maha Vairocana Temple, which was established in 2000.

Foreword

"Every society, every club, every business has its secrets. Only if you're a full-blown member of that club can you get on the inside and share in its secrets. Maybe it's just a secret handshake, but maybe it's trade secrets that will allow you advantages that no one on the outside could even imagine.

Through this book: *The Top Secrets that Successful Real Estate Investors Don't Tell You,* it will be as though you are a member of clubs of successful real estate investors, and you will get the secrets, priceless lessons, and extraordinary insight from the great experience from worldwide real estate investment success.

In real estate investing, success greatly depends upon experience. Having the experience of those who came before you is invaluable. Without it, if you rely solely on the lessons from your own experience, making many more mistakes is inevitable.

No one can know everything even if you're smart, have multiple college degrees, or are experienced.

To better respond to difficulties or disasters ahead, ones that other real estate investors have already faced, you may find useful knowledge by relying on others' experience, helping you achieve new successes, learn from the mistakes of others will help you avoid failure and ultimately take you to the top.

What *Secrets to The Top Secrets that Successful Real Estate Investors Don't Tell You* reveals is that you can start with nothing: no money and no experience and end up with the world in the palm of your hand. You are given the information, valuable lessons to discover the right path for you. You will invest in real estate the smart way and achieve the success you desire.

In short, this book is the most complete summary of advice in the real estate business that has ever been collected. It has completed its mission: to provide you with useful advice to help you plan for your own success in real estate investing. Whether you are active or new to the real estate business, you will learn a lot from this book - *The Top Secrets that Successful Real Estate Investors Don't Tell You.*

Raymond Aaron
New York Times Best-selling Author

PART I

SIX STEPS TO BECOME
A SUCCESSFUL INVESTOR

Chapter 1

Start from Scratch

When we took refuge in the United States of America along with our family in the 1990s, we were not only penniless, but also in a difficult spot. We were both too old to attend high school and, at the same time, not qualified enough to enter university.

We possessed neither qualifications nor experiences, especially when there was a language barrier that prevented us from properly communicating in daily life. In those early years, we, along with thousands of other Vietnamese people who were making the first settlements, had to do whatever we could in order to survive and simultaneously find the time to go to school.

After a period of hard work, we were able to save small sums of money as we waveringly walked towards the business path. After luckily gaining success with some initial investments, we promoted all we had in hand for the purpose of garnering even greater successes.

Poorer than beggars

However, our aggressive and inexperienced youth led to the sudden bankruptcy of our business, losing everything in a fraction of the time it took to build. Especially when our first child was about to be born, our family fell into a more critical situation financially.

Without certifications, apart from the ability to trade, we basically had no practical skills. This first failure made us realize that our weakness stemmed from our lack of knowledge in the business world. So, we rushed into researching ways to do business, as well as finding jobs at the New York Life insurance company and the Coldwell Banker real estate agency. We have learned from many great experiences at these places, especially at New York Life insurance company. The skills that we were given here were very useful to us in future successes.

After that, we decided to leave our jobs at New York Life to concentrate on real estate investments in order to fulfill our long-term goals.

Fortunately, after some time, we were able to garner a bit of success, as we were able to purchase some real estate properties and build up some companies.

However, in 2006, a wrong business decision handed us our second failure; we had to sell out the clothing import company, transferred 90% of stocks of the real estate investment company and 100% stocks of the phone company, yet we still owed our business partners more than two million dollars.

The situation at that time was even worse than our first failure. The fact that we had big debt, while our two remaining companies were unable to earn enough to pay for staff's salaries, had left us totally penniless.

The wonder of having faith

Losing all assets, we were burdened with a debt that amounted to $2,000,000 – not a "small" amount in the context of life-and-death of our family at that time.

We must admit, during those years we were always skeptical about the belief to get rich from scratch. We sometimes bitterly thought that trading to earn every cent to pay our debt and raise three children was already a tough task; how could we dream about becoming rich? The lack of trust, the uncertainty, and the disappointment lasted until the time when we accidentally came across a book by Donald Trump – a billionaire real estate developer – in which he said that his business had also gone badly with a debt amounting to 9 billion dollars, yet after a few years, he was able to pay all his debts and become a billionaire again.

A little bit of faith was flickering in our mind, and then we searched for books on real estate investors and other rich people all over the world. We were flabbergasted to learn that most of the billionaires and millionaires throughout the world had one thing in common; they had experienced bankruptcy once or twice in life. Robert Kyosaki, a millionaire, a real estate investor and the author of the "Rich Dad Poor Dad" series of motivational books, once went into bankruptcy then bounced back to being a millionaire. Li Ka-Shing, a Hong Kong business magnate and a real estate investor, faced financial hardship in the early 1980s, yet he still managed to be rich again and is currently a multi-billionaire. Many other similar stories can be found everywhere.

Having read and witnessed the living proof of real people with real experiences had definitely fueled our drive to one day achieve that kind of success. As Archimedes soundly cried out "Eureka" when finding the famous law bearing his name, we felt the thumping of our hearts beating with a fierce belief that we would be rich once again. Compared to the situation of Donald Trump, our financial burden all of a sudden seemed very minimal in comparison.

So, we strengthened our beliefs and relied on them as a source of motivation to dedicate ourselves day and night in order to achieve our goal. With a strong sense of belief and the gained knowledge through the years, we were able to put this knowledge to good use in the real world. Gradually, this brought in some small but good results, which gave us tremendous encouragement. Stemming from the fact that we had faced many difficulties along the way, getting rich from scratch was definitely a difficult task, and even more so from a negative perspective of a few million dollars in debt.

Many times, we were discouraged as we stumbled upon obstacles. Also, we learned many expensive lessons in the next several years, yet we were still able to firmly keep our beliefs and patiently continued to step forward.

Finally, we were compensated for the hardships we had experienced when we managed to cross over the other side with real assets worth more than one million U.S. dollars.

If you always hold on to your beliefs, are patient, hard working, and ready to learn, then you will definitely be successful.

This was our only asset, which served as a foundation for us to build up from the difficult times in the past to the success we have today.

We have faith and beliefs that, whatever we can do, you can also do.

You can start from ground zero

We are among thousands of millionaires in the USA, who easily got rich from real estate. We believe that, if you have enough trust and a desire to be rich at the absolute level, then whatever your financial situation is, you can easily become a millionaire.

Fortunately, these methods and strategies worked out well for us, as well as many other people. There is no reason for you not to achieve your dreams if you are willing to take your time to learn so you can get the things that you want.

According to Forbes magazine in 2007, 46% of the millionaires in the USA were from the real estate sector and most of them were independent, having nothing but empty hands at the starting point.

Millionaires were able to build up from scratch, and so can you.

Believe that no one is better than you and no one is smarter than you. After 15 years of working and meeting many millionaires in the world, we realize one common thing is that most of them are not extraordinary at all; they are just ordinary people who work hard, know how to save money, and show their proficiency in their fields of investment, as well as never give up when faced with difficult situations.

Experience is the best teacher

In real estate investment, people, time, or owners may change, but experiences and investment skills last forever.

There is good news! These skills and experiences are something that you can learn.

In this book, you will learn about the experiences and skills of successful investors, and these will help you wherever you are, even when deep in debt, to the point where you are financially stable.

Once you have gained enough experience, real estate investment will become much more manageable. Investing in real estate is already an easy way to become wealthy, thus when combined with the skills, strategies, and experiences of predecessor investors, this process of becoming wealthy will be readily available to everyone.

Chapter 2
Why Real Estate Investment
Makes It Easy to Become a Millionaire

There are thousands of reasons you can become rich with real estate investment, but for unique reasons why it is an *easy* way for anyone to become rich, we invite you to take a look at the following:

Simple Business Model

With a common business model, if a company wants to implement its business activities in an effective way, it requires the cooperation of everyone involved, and has to endure significant pressure from its customers on a daily and hourly basis. Investing in real estate, you do not need to worry as much. You can choose to hire assistants if you want; however, you can also conduct business by yourself if you so desire. You can repair the house and manage the tenants yourself, or you can simply buy real estate and live there while you wait for its value to increase.

We can predict that there are a lot of millionaires that are similar to a couple that we have known in the Bay Area. When they immigrated to America in 1983, they spent their total savings of $25,000 to buy a house to reside in. It was a newly-built house with a price tag of $220,000.

They lived in this house for 20 years up until 2003. As they got older, they did not want to carry out the difficult task of cleaning a two-storey house. Therefore, they sold it in favor of a smaller one. As a result, they became millionaires.

As you see, with a simple business model like that, anyone, regardless of their age, occupation, or intelligence can easily conduct such a business.

Growth in Population and Wealth

According to the statistics of the world population, on average the population increases by 74 million per year. In 1805, the total world population was 1 billion people and that number has reached 7 billion by 2013. If the population continues to steadily increase up until 2050, then the world's population will be 11 billion people.

New human beings are born continuously; however, land is not expandable. As a result, it will become scarcer and more expensive in the future because everyone needs a place to stay. Once the population increases too much, and there is not enough land for the mass population, there will definitely be a rise in constructing multi-storey buildings, skyscrapers, or even digging deeply into the ground. At that time, your small piece of land will significantly increase in value as the population continues to grow.

Anyone who has been to Hong Kong has a preview of the outlook of the future. The price of land there is one of the most expensive in the world, but they still hustle to have a place to live. They have to build multi-storey buildings and skyscrapers, where hundreds and thousands of families live together on such a small parcel of land.

This situation will also affect big established cities such as: London, New York, Tokyo, Paris…

Inflation

Twenty years ago, with $250,000, you could buy a newly-built 3,000 sq ft house in the Bay Area, but now you need anywhere from $800,000 to $1,000,000 to purchase a similar house.

And we believe that, 20 years from now, our children will need at least $1,500,000 or more to purchase a new home in this area.

Over time, inflation will increase the price of everything.

Housing property is considered the best asset that benefits from inflation, partially because its value is increased due to the cost of construction (labor) and the supplies (material) being inflated, and also because of the strengths of financial leverage.

When you invest in gold or stock, if you have $25,000, you can only buy the value of such items, at their true value. But for real estate investment, with that same amount, you could buy a property at $250,000 or even $500,000.

Then, when inflation occurs (assuming 3%), you only benefit from the amount of the investment in gold or stock at $25,000 (i.e. for the invested amount in gold of $25,000 in a year, you will get a profit of $25,000 x 3 % = $750).

Whereas, in real estate investment, the difference is that you enjoy the inflation not only from the deposited amount of $25,000, but also from the property value (i.e. you profit from the inflation rate of 3% of the $225,000 you borrowed from the bank). That means that, for the amount of $25,000 in a year, the real estate investment will benefit you ($25,000 + $225,000) x 3 % = $7500.

With the same invested amount, but for investment in real estate, you can benefit 30% by inflation, whereas for gold investment, you get a paltry sum of only 3%.

Tax Advantages

Property ownership benefits from taxes more than other investment sectors. All relevant expenses such as interest paid to the bank and the costs of insurance, lawyer fees, asset manager, repair, losses, depreciation and amortization over time shall be deducted. Also, when you visit your properties for lease away from your home, expenses for car, airline tickets, and hotel stays shall be excluded, whereas for investment in gold and stock, you will not be entitled to such preferences.

Another advantage is that, when you want to sell a property, you gain big earnings and have no obligation to immediately pay tax for such earnings, so you can apply for the 1031 Exchange program to delay the time for paying that tax and use such earnings to buy another property. Then, you continue to delay paying tax due to your earning and use the amount obtained from the delay in paying tax to buy another house. And you can continue this trend until you want to pay tax or, if not, you can use that amount of money for the rest of your life.

Are you excited about that? We, ourselves, felt very happy when we first saw the benefits of property investors.

BUT WHY ARE PEOPLE NOT RICH?

If buying properties can generate such easy successes, then why are there so few people who are rich? According to the statistics reported by the IRS, only 3-10% of the population is rich.

If an average couple in a normal workforce can still become millionaires (see the introduction), then anyone who is ambitious enough can become rich. But why are the majority of people still not rich?

Here are four reasons:.

First Reason: AWARENESS OF THE OPPORTUNITIES.

The top reason is that they have never thought or believed that they could afford to own a house to live in, let alone believe that they could become rich from real estate investment.

After 15 years of investing and communicating with thousands of first-time home buyers, we discovered that a lot of people can actually buy a house within and beyond what they can afford, but still do not believe that they can own a house for themselves.

Because they assume that they cannot afford to own a property, they do not think about or find out how to own it. If someone does not have any desire to own a house, then it is nearly impossible for them to want to invest in real estate in order to become rich.

So, the first reason why people do not become millionaires with real estate investment is that the desire to own properties and get rich from real estate has never crossed their minds and, of course, if they have never come up with the idea, they will never take any necessary steps to make it a reality.

Second Reason: DECISION

Another reason why people do not become rich in the real estate field is that they have never decided on actually purchasing properties in which to invest. Even though they have read many books on how to invest, attended workshops about investments or collaborated with real estate investors, these activities will not change anything until they make the decisions to buy properties for themselves.

Despite the fact that the desire to become rich through investment has crossed their minds, if they do not decide to take the first step of being a property owner, then they are just merely treading water.

One of the main reasons for not becoming rich in real estate investment is that most people do not take that first step in making the investment a reality. They have never firmly decided on or are certain that they will become a rich landlord. They only expect, intend, hope, and pray that they will own many houses and become rich one day, but never definitively decide to purchase any property.

The decision to move forward is the most important step for building a stable platform for the future.

Third Reason: PROCRASTINATION

Procrastination can prevent people from becoming rich. People always come up with reasons not to start doing what they know needs to be done in order to become homeowners. They always think that it is not the right time, or the opportunity has not ripened yet ... or they are not eligible, cannot afford to buy houses ... or the market is not as good as they desire ... prices may be too high, resulting in the fact that they cannot afford to purchase, and they are also possibly at risk, or nothing is guaranteed ... or perhaps they just have to patiently wait...

It seems that there are always reasons to procrastinate, so they continue to put it off one month after another, and then years pass before they realize that it is too late.

Although the desire to become an investor, own a property, and deciding that they need a change has crossed their mind, their delay will alter all of their plans indefinitely. Procrastination has taken away the opportunity to acquire wealth and affluence that was once within their fingertips.

Fourth Reason: LIVING FRUGALLY

Successful investors usually mention the fact that amateur investors do not wait until their investment has reached their intended targets, but they often "squeeze money out of their houses" to spend lavishly on luxury expenses. That is another reason for real estate owners to fall into insolvency or bankruptcy, or fail to achieve the wealth that they had hoped for.

Their future wealth has gone up in smoke when they withdraw their equities from the houses to spend, live lavishly, buy cars and other expensive items, leading to the impossible reduction in the house-related debts, and such debts will only increase as each day passes.

A tree has just begun to grow and has not fully blossomed into fruit yet, but its branches are then suddenly chopped. With such bareness, how it can have enough vitality to develop and grow?

When the potential in real estate has yet to multiply, but its vitality is taken away, the profitability of the investment will take much longer to occur.

If you cannot suppress your impulses and are forced to spend the equities from your houses, you will not become wealthy.

To become a successful and wealthy investor in the future, skills, a sure means of frugality, and saving habits must be applied. If you do not have these foundations, it will be difficult for you to reach that level of affluence.

By the time you realize that your career lies in your decision, and once you take that leap of faith, you will be on your way to affluence.

Before going too in-depth about the successful methods used by professional real estate investors, we need to get a good grasp of the "six steps to become a successful real estate investor."

Chapter 3

Six Steps to Become
A Successful Real Estate Investor

To succeed in investing, you have to learn the essential skills to succeed. The prosperity of the investment is not a matter of luck, but the core factors for the successes are your knowledge, skills, and the application of your combined knowledge and skills. Nowadays, your success in investment can be achieved regardless of where your starting point is, your non-existent knowledge, or inexperience in investment. Each of these essential skills leading to success in investment can actually be learned.

If you have done what we did, and researched about the experiences of thousands of stories of successful millionaires and investors, you will discover many remarkable points. You can find an amazing similarity in all successful millionaires' ways and steps to achieve affluence in all the cases. People are rich thanks to their thriving business, investment in various properties, and other services...but most of them have walked on the same very familiar road. They all put forward a plan and used the same skills to jump-start their careers.

Some people have raised the question as to whether all the successful people had gone through the same steps to get rich. Therefore, under careful analysis, are we able to generalize those common skills and refer to them for future references? The answer is…YES!

So, let's find out and learn the skills to become successful real estate investors.

The following are the most fundamental ones; each represents one essential skill to be thoroughly mastered for anyone desiring to become a successful investor in real estate:

STEP 1:
Possess the mindset of a successful investor

How is real estate investment related to the mindset of an investor?

If you just want to become a mediocre investor then you do not need to find out more about this step; however, if you start from scratch and want to become a successful investor and to maintain that success even through the turmoil of the economy and become even more prosperous one day, then this is the basic knowledge that you need to have a good grasp on.

An experienced investor once told us that successful people develop their ability to predict great opportunities in places amateur investors presumed to be problematic areas.

The successful people are no different than us; however, their desire to learn, their practice, and their past experiences throughout the years have helped set them apart from the crowd.

In Chapter 4, you will get acquainted with the habits of successful investors. Once you have acquired those habits and the methods to build a strong foundation, you will discover numerous opportunities all around you, without having to look far away. You will start noticing opportunities just next door that you never realized were there.

STEP 2:
Determine a Specific Investment Strategy

There's a saying that "the success in investing in real estate is seen right at the time of purchasing the property, not at the time of selling." Successful investors are aware of their victories immediately after buying properties, rather than knowing their profits after waiting 5 to 10 years or until the time the property is sold. They are winners right from the beginning.

A specific strategy or plan is not often set up by most amateur investors before investing. Due to this lack of planning, they can easily be rattled if the economy is on a downfall, and this can eventually lead them to give up entirely.

It is partly the reason why many people continue to participate in making investments while real estate prices skyrocket. When there are fluctuations and reductions in the housing prices, these can elevate a sense of fear in the amateur investors that can lead them to withdraw and flee for their lives, resulting in a non-stop drop in the housing prices.

To achieve such successes, before making decisions on an investment, it is necessary to develop a specific strategy and plan to avoid the uncertainty of the growth of the economic market and the sense of insecurity by the decline of the real estate market. Even when faced with difficult situations, smart investors can still calmly fight on because everything will unfold smoothly under their strategies and plans.

The strategies as well as principles for a successful plan will be shown in Chapters 5 and 6; thereby, an appropriate path can be considered and chosen to suit your capital, talent, experience, and situation.

Once you choose the right strategy for your target and situation and you stick to such a strategy throughout the investment path until your target is achieved, you will find your investment to be an interesting process, and not dangerous at all.

STEP 3:
Select the Right Properties for Potential Investment

The process of selecting the potential targeted property is to choose the one matching your investment strategies. Each year, millions of houses are traded many times in the United States. You cannot select all or any kind of property, but you can select the appropriate one to meet your targets. Our main aim is to become successful and wealthy; therefore, selecting the property to achieve our anticipated goals is of great importance. We do not need to spend time tracking all real estate trades in the market or participate in any business affairs, if it is not consistent with your goals.

Chapters 8 and 9 will show you the fundamental knowledge to choose a property, how to evaluate it, and the principles to start safe and highly profitable investments, thereby building your own investment system.

STEP 4:
Increase Value of Real Estate

Selecting a good property is the beginning of a successful investment process. However, the increase in investment value of new real estate is a big step to becoming very successful in this field.

In Chapter 11, you will learn about the stories of successful investors and about how they spectacularly increased their real estate. Also, this chapter will show you the basic steps to improve your investment in the initial process. As a result, you will understand why successful investors can boost their investment properties in such a rapid way.

STEP 5:
Manage Investment Capitals and Debts

Many people think that selecting a good property and raising their investment value to make that property exponentially grow is the goal. But in fact it is only half of the ladder to becoming wealthy. A lot of people have good ideas and have chosen good real estate for investment, and also give good suggestions to promote the investment value in an unexpected way. But on the subsequent track, most of them rejoiced over their victories and neglected in the inspection and management of their invested capital. And the unexpected events cost them a large amount of money to fix those mistakes, or any uncertainty caused by poor inspection and management of the invested properties. To avoid landing in that situation, you should know which items are required to be inspected and managed in the process of the investment.

In Chapter 12, you will learn several mandatory rules and conditions that any investor who wants to be successful must practice and apply regularly.

STEP 6:
Repeat or Expand Your Victories

Globally-known companies such as Wal-Mart, McDonald's, KFC, and the mega-rich at an international scale have proven this formula. They successfully opened the first store, and their second, third... even 1,000th stores based on the successful experience of the first one, thereby rapidly multiplying their assets. And so can you! When you gain success, just repeat it time and time again. Successful investment is the key to becoming a large-scale business and having a booming career in real estate trading. This will also be a stepping stone towards a wealthy future.

Special attention should be paid to the repetition of your victories and development of your successful opportunities to make them become bigger over time.

These are the six necessary steps to become a successful investor in the real estate field. Now, let's study each step thoroughly and start with the habits of the millionaires.

In this chapter, we will discover the successful investor's way of thinking. This is also the first step in the wealth-making formula of the 6-step success.

PART II

SECRETS OF INVESTORS
WHO HAVE BECOME MILLIONAIRES

Chapter 4

Six Thinking Habits of Successful Investors

What are the thinking habits of a successful person? The thinking here is understood as the way we view the objective world. That's how we shape, screen, and perceive our experiences. Maybe you and I experienced the same event, but we may have very different perspectives. That is because we have different ways of thinking, thus leading to different actions and results. Let me give you an example: When reading an advertisement of a certain product that may have the opportunity to make money, what do you think of? What do you feel? And what's your response to it?

One: do not pay attention to it.

Two: Oh! That's just silly.

Three: this advertisement is quite good. But just stop there and promptly forget it.

Yes, what you do depends on your thinking. Most people consider it a normal advertisement for reading purposes only.

But what will people with successful thinking do?

James W. Walter, a millionaire, the owner of Jim Walter Homes and Walter Industries, the second largest company in housing construction sector in the U.S. in the 1980s, encountered a similar situation in 1956. He read an advertisement in the local paper about the so-called "shell" homes. It was a structure in which a company would be responsible for building the "shell" of the house while the customer would complete the interior details at their will. He found that it was a housing-related workaround for people with little money. During that time, a large number of soldiers demobilized after World War II came back home, and they needed a place to live at a fairly low price. After folding up the paper, he met and convinced constructors to cooperate with him in the construction and selling of cheap houses on a large scale. Ultimately, that was the premise that made his company the second largest construction company in the United States, and the one that built most of the houses during that time.

The notable idea here is that, from just a small advertisement, James Walter used his brain to develop a great business that reaps in a lot of money.

So, if you are not successful now, it suggests that you have not followed the correct path. In other words, if you want to change your life, then you should do things differently. To do so, you should have a different way of thinking. And the mindset of successful individuals is expressed in their own habits, faith, values, and attitudes.

Now, let's find out the "6 habits of successful real estate investors". Once you possess these habits, money will smoothly flow in your direction. In contrast, without having a grasp of these habits, you will be going in circles trying to invest without much success.

Habit #1 of a Successful Investor:
ALWAYS EAGER TO LEARN

"Turn everything touched into gold."

Maybe, you've heard others compare professional investors, who acquire one success after another, to someone who can turn almost everything they touch into gold. Some people feel astonished and assume that those people were born with a magical touch.

However, successful real estate investors would argue that the ability to bring such great successes is not innate or naturally handed to them, but is because they have been continuously learning new and improved things. They then have to improve themselves by diligently practicing and modifying what they have learned in their daily lives, which in turns help lead them on the right path filled with opportunities.

Donald Trump said: "Finance and business are often compared to the dangerous seas where vicious sharks are always lurking and are eager to devour the prey, i.e. innocent novices. In this game, knowledge is the key to success".

His words reminded me, Kim, of the business experience of my paternal family, which has been deeply ingrained in my mind since I was very young.

From the time I was about 10 years old, my paternal family had a sawmill specializing in the production of wooden cabinets and doors in Saigon, VietNam. The sawmill was doing very well at that time. My whole paternal family, including my uncles, aunts, and cousins, was involved in this sawmill business. My uncles and father were responsible for the production and management of the workers, while my aunts took care of the finances and sales, and my cousins were responsible for the public relations of the business.

However, by the late 1980s, things had started to change; production significantly reduced due to slow and sluggish sales. I was too young to comprehend the condition of the market, so I wondered if our products were not as good compared to other businesses'. But, after visiting the neighboring sawmills, I saw that they were also closing stores and reducing the number of employees. I wondered what significant changes were happening and why the big sawmills all around the region had slumped in sales.

Later on, as an adult and after researching, I realized that human tastes had changed. Wooden doors and other wooden furniture at that time gradually ceased to be popular and were replaced by ironwork, which was the new favored material. My family's sawmill did not adapt in time with the current trend; it quickly went downhill and into bankruptcy. The rapid transformation of the market had pushed my family's sawmill out of business and forced my entire family into a difficult transformation of their lives.

My grandparents' sawmill is just one small example of the market changes over time. If you look to the past, you will see a lot of great careers and businesses ruined according to the change of tastes of the market when an era passes through to another. We do not have to look far away; we just look back in the last 10 years. When the electronic era changed to the internet era, millions of emails were sent quickly every day without the need to spend money on postage and letters. This pushed the post office sector, a giant industry with hundreds of years of history, down unexpectedly.

Everything will change in time. Depending on the industry, that change can be fast or slow. Like any business, investment real estate can change too. Although real estate preferences do not change as rapidly as other businesses, these changes depend on consumer spending habits, mortgage interest rates, unemployment rates, and the new rules, which are changing quickly. If investors do not capture the changes of the market, do not learn to acquire new knowledge and fall behind, they risk not only losing momentum in their business investments, but also possible legal consequences if they do not pay attention to or ignore the laws.

To become a successful real estate investor, it is crucial to save some funds in order to acquire more knowledge by regularly reading books, newspapers, and magazines, and by attending seminars to improve yourself, as well as do more research than other investors do. This will help you firmly establish your position despite any changes in the market.

We have heard a saying from somewhere that "Every morning in Africa, a gazelle wakes up; it knows that it must out run the fastest lion or it will be killed. Every morning in Africa, a lion wakes up; it knows it must run faster than the slowest gazelle, or it will starve".

It doesn't matter whether you are the lion or a gazelle; when the sun comes up; you'd better be running...

Habit #2 of a Successful Investor:
ALWAYS PLAN BEFORE INVESTING

Successful investors always envision their territories before they set them up. So, they always prepare plans for the step-by-step achievement of their desired goals. Similarly, before investing in any property, they draft a project plan. Such plans will tell them:

- For what purposes did they buy the properties?
- How long will they hold on to or sell their properties?
- How much profit will they want to get out of their properties?

Amateur investors do this in the opposite way. They rarely have clear figures and purposes, but always follow their gut feelings about the market. When house prices are skyrocketing, everyone is scrambling to buy houses. They suppose that the market is safe since there are many other house buyers. So, they immediately jump into the market just as they worry about being displaced and losing out on the opportunities to reap in profits from the increasing market if they do not join it at that time.

Then, when the market hits rock bottom, housing prices drop miserably, their debts are higher than the value of the houses, and they retreat and leave behind the invested assets they have saved their entire lives.

Professional investors are less likely to do so. Although, sometimes, they also make a few wrong predictions and their properties are not worth much, they still persevere and are not too worried or in a state of panic to sell off the properties in which they invested, because they have already had a clear plan. They know when to sell their houses and when to earn profits from such properties before investing their money in real estate.

Preparing a business plan before making any purchase is an important habit for you, so as to see an overall picture of the investment like a roadmap for a journey.

The plan for success will help you know where you are, what you need to do, and how long it takes to reach the destination. With a plan, your journey will become much smoother. Also, it brings you a peace of mind and helps you feel assured so you can boldly step forward to make your dreams come true.

If you do not have any plans, you will not know when you reach the destination, where you are, or whether you are going up to the North Pole or are going down to the South Pole, or any other place on Earth.

It is also the key for you to decide whether to buy a certain property or not right, before spending your hard-earned money on it. Making an appropriate plan will help you save time, money, energy, and make a quick decision to grasp the opportunities so as to achieve the best results.

Lucas – a successful real estate investor in Alameda – said that in an auction of real estate in court in 1997, he made a bid for a piece of land, which was a small island in Contra Costa County. At that time, a 12-acre island was sold at US$95,000. That was the highest price for the land, uninhabited and full of wild plants.

Lucas recounted that the price of the land at that time was relatively high. However, Lucas had a long-term investment plan. He would develop housing construction on that land in the future so, for him, the price was still low. Lucas was not afraid to pay a higher price to buy that piece of land on the island. And his plan came to reality.

In 2003, he constructed over 100 new houses around the island shore. Today, his small island is an ideal residential area for those who love the sea and fishing, as well as those wanting to own large yachts anchored behind their houses.

Preparing a plan before investing will help you quickly make the right decisions from the start, and bring you opportunities that investors without a plan cannot grasp.

Habit #3 of a Successful Investor: FREQUENTLY DEDICATE TIME TO SURVEY THE MARKET

Many investors that start their real estate investments usually neglect the importance of thoroughly surveying the market on a regular basis. Due to this negligence, it is very easy to stumble upon mistakes. Real estate investment is a very important matter that is worth a huge amount of money. Thus, if you do not have a clear understanding of the market before plunging yourself into this field, you can easily fall prey to the ubiquitous traps.

The market is continuously changing, and even though the market for real estate does not fluctuate as fast as the stock market, many events can occur on a daily basis that can significantly affect the value of your real estate. These events can range anywhere from companies going bankrupt ... to new companies being established ... public transportation ... new tax laws ... schools and new business plazas ... or just simply new projects in your local area...

This is a lesson learned from one of our investor friends. After the success of a real estate developer in Santa Clara, he decided to buy many lots of land in order to build an apartment complex with 120 units. In the meantime, there was another company nearby that commenced their construction of two apartment complex towers with 350 units. In the midst of his construction, the other company had just completed their project, had rented out 50% of their total units, and was aggressively advertising to rent out the rest of their units. Once the construction for our friend's complex finished, even with many strategic advertising methods, he could rent out only 15% of the units, and there was no demand for the remaining units. After several months of leaving the units empty, he eventually went into bankruptcy.

The lesson learned from our friend is that he did not have a full grasp of the demand for apartments in the area that he was constructing in. There were only 200 units for rent per year, while the other apartment complex had 350 units, thus they needed one and a half to two years in order to rent out all their units. Therefore, it is not too hard to understand the low demand for the number of units remaining at our friend's apartment complex.

Some people assume that only large investors feel the need to investigate the market, whereas there is no need to carefully research the market when you just want to buy one or two real estate properties.

Real estate investment has to do with a huge sum of money; even if it is just one or two properties, they are still worth a significant amount. If you do not have a full grasp of the market, you might purchase real estate to invest when the price is very high. Or you were planning to rent out the property to the workers of a factory, but the factory suddenly decided to relocate, what are you going to do?

Having a complete understanding of the market not only helps prevent risky situations in this investment game, it can also help you purchase real estate that has the potential to bring in high profits.

A tiger that wants to capture a deer always sits back and surveys the area in order to seize the right opportunity to attack. Therefore, professional investors suggest that, if you want to become successful in real estate, you need to be able to predict and have full access to the important information in order to prevent any possible mistakes. In addition, you need to seize the opportunity so that you can achieve your goal quickly and precisely.

Habit #4 of a Successful Investor:
LONG-SIGHTED VISION

There is a story of two brothers named Mac and Mai in Myanmar. Each of them has inherited from their father a nice piece of land in the center of a prosperous city. Before handing over the land, the father had enclosed a clause in his will as follows: "These pieces of land are for building houses to live in or business purposes and are not for sale." After receiving the inheritance, they wanted to move there and decided to build houses on their pieces of land.

The older brother, Mac, built a grand 2-storey house with the facade of four tall round pillars propping up the bright red tile roofs, highlighting the surrounding luxurious balconies.

Meanwhile, his younger brother, Mai, also built a 2-storey house but in a different way. His house looked like an upturned square black box with no tiles on the roof but a flatly coated cement layer, making his house less appealing.

Mac always laughed at Mai and quietly boasted of his intelligence.

A few years later, Mai built four more storeys and turned his previous ugly box into a six-storey modern hotel surrounded by blue glass walls. After that, the hotel became an automatic money-making machine when he rented it out to a professional for business purposes. He only kept a room for himself and travelled around the world with no worries about money for the rest of his life.

The story tells us that Mai had a long-sighted vision of 20 to 50 years whereas Mac only had a long-sighted vision of about 10 to 20 years.

Each person has his own vision, which often determines his fortune and status. As Brian Tracy once said, "The average professional person has a vision of 10, 15, 20 years or longer, while a normal person in the workforce has a long-sighted vision of about two pay periods. Often, the vision of people who are at the bottom of the society -- runabouts, drug addicts, or alcoholics -- are only hours or even minutes."

Successful people always have plans and long-sighted vision of 20 to 50 years, and even as far as a few generations.

German Prince Albert Von Thurn is well known as a wealthy owner of three hundred thousand hectares of vast forests in Europe, a technology plant, an expensive collection, and a castle with five hundred rooms in Regent Berlin. These assets were inherited from his family's properties bought from centuries earlier.

Similarly, the richest British billionaire, Gerald Cavendish, inherited US$14 billion from centuries ago. In the 1600s, his family bought a cheap corn farm, and hundreds of acres of cabbage land, which are currently very expensive properties as they are in the center of London.

Immigrants who came to the United States empty-handed worked hard and went through much sacrifice in order for their children to excel in school; this selfless act by the parents demonstrated their long-sighted vision, whether their investment paid off or not. However, the more important lesson is their belief that they can improve the future of their children, grandchildren, and other generations to come.

The incredible sacrifice and foresight of such parents has given their children and future generations a chance of having a bright future. Previous generations' foresight can make changes and create a solid foundation for future generations.

To achieve the success you want, you should think about not only today, but also an investment in 5, 10, or 20 years' time or longer.

Life is not always smooth sailing. None can guarantee that you will be successful, live peacefully, and obtain such great stability throughout your life. Failures, losses, and accidents are common occurrences in life and are unfortunately inevitable, regardless of your wealth or status.

The thought of day-to-day working is a hindering habit that remains a barrier to your goal to become rich. Without foresight, preparation for uncertainties such as economic slowdown, unemployment or any changes, you will not know what to do to escape from the impasse. Similarly, if you are not prepared to seize any upcoming opportunities, such as a 50% discount on a certain property, then you also do not know how to garner success.

> **The power of foresight and preparation for uncertainties and opportunities in the future are the essential habits for those who want to be successful and wealthy.**

With a long-sighted and long-term vision, you are more likely to set bigger goals and complete long-term plans. You will think more maturely, and you will develop a greater sense of patience and perseverance until you achieve your ultimate goals. So, from now on, you should extend your vision. Everything you're doing today should be considered as a part of a long-term process of your career. Even if you do not become rich, it can certainly help you become more financially prosperous.

This is the will of the people who constantly go forward and achieve great success in their lifetime.

Habit #5 of a Successful Investor:
HABIT OF UTILIZING MONEY

The habit of spending is the most important habit, and it is also a very special habit that you need to be efficient in. This habit not only helps bring you great fortune in the future or provides you with the financial security in real estate investments, it can lead to success in any other branches that you may pursue.

So, what are spending habits?

You have heard stories of lottery winners that have dwindled their fortune just after several years and they find themselves in the same financial condition as before the big win. Those instances are proof that those people do not possess good spending habits.

So what are good spending habits?

Good spending habits consist of turning your hard-earned money into even bigger amounts every day, instead of making it disappear overtime. In order to do so, successful investors have a habit of restricting themselves to various *saving methods, reinvestments,* and have a specified amount of *money saved up for emergencies.*

1. Savings

Every time the thought of a wealthy or successful person enters people's minds, they usually think of someone who is elegant, covered in brand-names from head to toe complete with extravagant jewelry pieces, and someone who lives in a marvelous house with yachts and private jets.

In all honesty, those are just images depicted in movies, television shows, and magazines. In reality, wealthy and successful people do not usually live like that.

In the book, "The Millionaire Next Door" Thomas J. Stanley, who has interviewed over 300 wealthy individuals in the world, realized an ironic notion: elegant folks who drive exotic cars, don very expensive clothing, and appear to have endless amounts of money usually do not have a lot of money in their accounts.

In contrast, people who actually have money in their accounts live very simply, drive old cars, and actually wear affordable clothing. Due to their special way of savings, they have generated a great level of wealth that is admired by many people.

Warren Buffet, a billionaire whose wealth is ranked 3rd in the world with a total of more than $42 billion dollars, has never owned a yacht, and currently lives in a moderate home that he purchased in 1958 with a price of $31,500 in Dundee, at the center of Omaha, Nebraska.

Ingvar Kamprad, the founder of the biggest wholesale furniture company, IKEA, has a fortune of $3 billion dollars. However, he still drives a Volvo 240 that was made in 1993 and regularly flies coach during his travels. According to an article by Reuters in 2006, in his home in Switzerland, the furniture that he uses is from IKEA and not some excessively extravagant furniture.

Sam Walton, the owner of a corporation specialized in wholesales, Wal-Mart, is among one of the wealthiest people in the world. He possesses 1,960 Wal-Mart stores, with over 380,000 employees, and brings in close to $50 billion annually. However, he still drives an old car, a 1979 Ford, and lives quietly in a small city in Arkansas.

In order to be successful and wealthy, people who are new to the investment field should always save up to accumulate a tremendous amount for the future.

2. Reinvestment

Accomplished investors have shared that their habits of reinvesting have helped them increase their fortune and success in a stable and rapid manner. They fully understand the phrase "money generates more money". Therefore, when they first start out, instead of living extravagantly like the majority of investors, they take the profits that they have made to purchase more real estate properties, which gradually increase over time.

The habit of reinvesting their profits has helped successful investors increase their properties rapidly and securely. They do not waste their money like the majority of other investors who buy fast cars or other expensive materialistic items that satisfy their cravings at the spur of the moment. They fully understand what it means to use money to generate even more money. Thus, they always reinvest in order to make their fortune prosper day after day.

There was once a farmer who had planted an apple tree. When it was time to harvest, he was only able to sell those apples to survive for several days. However, his dream was for every harvest season to not only last him several days, but for several years. He patiently followed his plan by using the seeds from the original tree to plant new ones. The farmer continued with this method for several years, which resulted in a forest of apple trees, instead of just a single tree. Now, he had to sit back and enjoy his fortune.

This is also the way that investors always utilize, which is buying more properties in order to establish the empire that they have always dreamt of.

Cultivate the habit of cleverly reinvesting, and one day you will see that your money has exponentially increased.

Reinvesting the profits garnered from initial investments in order to develop even further is an essential step when you start with empty hands or with limited funds if you want to become a successful and wealthy investor.

3. **Always have some money saved up in case of emergencies, and never rely on the income stemming from real estate investments.**

"Always be prepared with an amount of money needed to pay for 6 months of basic necessities for your family."

When an expert investor shared his experiences with us in 2000, we did not pay much attention to what he had to say. We were in a celebratory mood since we had a steady income stemming from the units that we were renting out and the profits coming from the two companies that we owned. However, when 2001 rolled around, the units that we were renting out had become vacant and the real estate business was also affected due to the stock market crash of 2000–2002. Business was not going well, and the income we were able to garner was not enough. That was when it hit us how important the expert investor's advice was.

The habit of relying on the income from real estate to survive can be detrimental because of what happens when the income starts to slow down and you are so used to spending extravagantly. When business slows down and money is tight, people tend to sell off their personal items and properties at a very low price in order to cover the basic necessities in their daily lives. This can cause you to feel mentally insecure. We adopted this advice, and it significantly helped our financial condition to become more secure and stable. Since our financial situation is stable, we also feel mentally secure and do not rush into making reckless decisions. This is because we do not feel pressured by the monthly basic necessities to sell off properties when they have not reached their full potential.

As you may already know, real estate investment can generate a lot of money at times, little money at other times, and sometimes does not yield any income at all. If you rely on it to survive or pay for your monthly basic necessities, then it can significantly affect your mentality. The thought of needing an income to cover your monthly expenses might cause you to make rash decisions and sell properties immediately during the time when the properties have not reached their full potential. It is similar to the times when you have lots of money and you are used to that way of spending; however, when you have no income, it will be very hard to refrain from spending, which causes you to dig into your capital funds.

Therefore, saving up enough money to survive for 6 months and live within your means will help you have a strong mentality. This will help you in making wise decisions, as you do not have to worry about monthly expenses, which can affect your real estate investments.

MONTHLY INVESTMENT OF $5,000, HOW LONG IT TAKES TO BECOME A BILLIONAIRE

By chance, at the age of 29, we researched if a person invests US$5,000 per month, how long it would take for him to become a billionaire.

The figures we came up with can be surmised as follows:

	15%	20%	25%	30%
5 years	$453,408	$522,270	$604,221	$701,956
10 years	$1,398,286	$1,916,817	$2,669,203	$3,768,420
20 years	$7,584,774	$15,812,396	$34,300,476	$76,621,282
30 years	$35,054,103	$116,809,008	$409,878,574	$1,486,917,903
40 years	$157,023,777	$850,878,137	$4,869,329,378	$28,787,651,192
50 years	$698,595,138	$6,186,279,748	$57,818,906,446	$557,279,336,777

We realized that if a person invests $5,000 per month regularly with an interest rate of 20% per year, he will become a billionaire after 41 years.

With such monthly investment at a regular interest rate of 25% per year, he will become a billionaire after only 34 years. Similarly, with interest rate of 30% per year, it will only take 29 years to become a billionaire.

Therefore, if you save an amount of money for regular investment, and invest that money, you should combine all principal and profit to reinvest, instead of taking the profit every year. In the following year, you should include the profit you earned into your capital and continue the investment.

Like the aforesaid example, with a monthly investment of $5,000, to become a millionaire:

- With an annual profit rate of 15%, you will take less than 9 years.
- With an annual profit rate of 20%, you will take less than 8 years.
- With an annual profit rate of 25%, you will take less than 7 years.
- With an annual profit rate of 30%, you will take less than 6 years.

This is called the power of compound interest. It is also the secret of the rich to acquiring more and more money. Thus, to become a rich person as you have hoped, you should learn how to invest and utilize money from successful investors. You should always save money and try to spend the remaining amount after extracting 10-15% of your salary for investment. With such extraction, you invest in properties at a profit rate of 8-15% or higher. You should carefully manage and control your investment so that it can increase by the hour and minute. By continuously doing so, we believe that, even if you cannot become a billionaire, you will certainly be a millionaire.

Chapter 5
Strategies to Successful Investments from Professional Investors

A professional investor once told us, "Real estate is like playing chess; in order to win, you need to have a good strategy, and this strategy needs to have a good plan. Therefore, you should write up a business plan before buying any real estate properties."

That advice helped us tremendously after hitting rock bottom in 2006, and helped us maintain our success during the real estate crisis in 2009.

If you talk to other investors who have unfortunately failed in their real estate investments, you will see that the majority of them are unprepared and do not have a plan carefully drawn up. Do not fall into this trap!

In contrast, professional investors always have a planned agenda before investing. In fact, they have drawn up a plan before investing in any real estate properties. They view *real estate investment as a business*; therefore, the road to achieving their ultimate goal is quite the journey. Thus, they simply cannot just guess where they are going in this journey.

Just take a second to think about this; if you hop in a car to travel to a completely foreign area that you have never set foot in before, would you just trust your instincts to start this journey or would you bring a map along with you? The majority of the people will choose to bring a map, iPhone, or any other tools that may help guide them in the correct direction.

The reason we use a map is to arrive to the destination via the simplest path, in the shortest amount of time, to avoid any detours, and especially to anticipate what will come up next on the road.

This principle is also utilized in this journey of real estate investments.

To have an agenda in real estate investment is a definite necessity. A good plan does not only transform your dream of being wealthy into reality, but it can also help in establishing a secure career for you in the future. It will definitely bring you much success and help achieve your ultimate goal with ease.

Besides that, another advantage that experienced investors have shared is that your business plan is a very beneficial tool when you apply for loans at the bank or when seeking a source of funding for the properties that you plan to buy.

Therefore, you should always develop a business plan; in fact you should have it fully drawn out before you even think about purchasing a property.

Without a good investment plan, it will be very hard to succeed even if you have grand ideas for your investments. Unfortunately, you will likely encounter failures in the process if you plunge into investing without a solid plan.

DRAW OUT THE PLAN TO BECOME
WEALTHY IN THE SHORTEST AMOUNT OF TIME

What do you imagine, starting from the time you begin your career in real estate investment to the day you become satisfied with the extent of your empire? You should just write it out on paper.

Ryan B. knows that buying and selling old houses will generate an enormous amount of profit. "I was fascinated with what the future held, but I was also very worried with the numerous details that came with this issue." He recalls, "When I planned out my agenda on paper I understood every step I needed to take was dependent on the time period. Also, I realized that the tasks I needed to do were much easier."

This is the agenda that Ryan B. has drawn out for himself:

1. Purchase an old home with a price of $300,000 and utilize the program for first-time home buyers to loan and make a down payment of $9000.
2. Repair the house and rent it out.
3. Increase the rent, then sell the house after.
4. With the profits garnered, buy a four-plex with four units.
5. Repeat the process of repairing and selling or go to the bank and increase the mortgage.
6. Use the profits from that to purchase more houses to repeat this process.

Ryan B. currently has 160 units for rent in three apartment complexes. The amount of rent he is able to collect each year is $1,260,000. The value of all his real estate properties totals up to $12,000,000.

It is understandable that Ryan B. will be overwhelmed to manage 160 units for rent, along with an asset valued up to $12,000,000. However, managing an old home is very plausible. Once you are able to manage that first step, you can definitely tackle the next one.

Now, we share Ryan B.'s experience of executing his plan with the purpose of demonstrating that your business plan does not have to be long or complicated.

Now, let's see what you need to do in order to develop an agenda to invest that fits your preferences.

STEP 1
Find out the reason you invest in real estate

People may say: Everyone knows that investing is to make money; what other reason is there?

Actually, money is just a side reason. What we want to focus on is the hidden reason behind your wanting to earn money or to become wealthy.

For example, Stephanie has strong feelings about the impoverished conditions that she had experienced in her early years. Her family was living in poverty, which led her father to become depressed because he felt helpless with the situation. Unfortunately, her father became addicted to alcohol and passed away when the family was still in the midst of crisis. Stephanie's mother worked in a restaurant in order to provide for her children. The rented home that they lived in was constantly being bombarded by the owner with reminders to pay their rent.

These events developed a sense of insecurity within Stephanie. She knows that *her goal in investing in real estate is to earn money to feel secure,* and to have a stable income so she does not have to worry about money for the rest of her life.

This has prompted Stephanie to choose to garner a steady income. Thus, Stephanie only focuses on small houses, and she immediately eliminates the overly expensive homes because those do not bring her the stable income she is looking for. In addition, Stephanie reveals that, with the amount of money that she puts out to buy an expensive home, she can buy 2 to 3 smaller houses to rent out in order to collect monthly rent money that is 2 to 3 times higher.

Steven is an active young man who has chosen to meet his goal of having $1 million dollars within a *short time span of 5 years.* Therefore, Steven is not selective as to whether a house is expensive or cheap; as long as the property brings in a plausible profit, he immediately will repair the home and sell it out.

As you can see, the reasons vary significantly for two different people. They will choose different products, as well as different paths and strategies to achieve their goals. Finding out the real reason behind your desire to invest will help you choose the right strategies that fit your preferences in order to reach the personal goals that you have set for yourself.

STEP 2:
Choose short-term or long-term

Determine whether you want to do this short-term or long-term depending on your goal.

-Short-term investment suggests that you buy or sell a property within a short period of time, anywhere from one month to one year.

Many investors use this strategy with the purpose of *earning quick money or expanding their assets with the money that they have.*

-Long-term investment is buying a property and keeping it for a long period of time, from 3 years and up. This is the most common way to invest. Investors use this method with the purpose of *waiting for the market to develop in the future, for an inflation that will decrease the money value, increase the value of their property, thereby earning a passive income coming from the monthly rent, or to reduce their taxes.*

It is your choice whether you want to invest short-term or long-term. The strategy that you choose will determine the price for which you buy property and how you execute your plan.

Now, you have to think about *whether you want to do short-term investment to increase your funds or whether you want to do long-term investment to gain passive income.*

STEP 3:
Choose a concrete goal

This is a story about a father and son in a desert:

One day at dusk, a father was lost in the desert when he went around looking for his son, who was also lost. The next morning, the son came back to camp, while the father was nowhere to be found. The son recalled the terrible experience when he was caught in the sandstorm and the severe conditions that he experienced at the time. Fortunately, *he knew exactly where he was, and his goal, and was determined to weather the sandstorm to come back home.* This eventually allowed him to return.

The father was going around trying to find his lost son, and he also became caught in the sandstorm. The main reason that led to the father's disappearance was his goal to find the person that was lost, *having no definite location he could pinpoint,* which led to his becoming totally lost.

When you fall in the pit of life, if you just aimlessly wander around, then you will not have any hopes and will most likely never escape from it. Many people believe that your courage and will can help you overcome the obstacles. However, if you cannot clearly *pinpoint your position and have no clear goals, then all the will that you have will become meaningless.*

In order to pinpoint your goal, you need to be able to answer the following questions:

- Where are you heading?
- What are you trying to get out of investing in real estate?
- Do you want to get a stable income of $10,000, $20,000 per month or do you want to reach $5,000,000, $10,000,000 within a timeframe?

In order for your goal to become a reality, you can fully summarize it with one word, SMART. S is Specific, M stands for Measureable, A for Achievable, R is Realistic, and T for Timely.

A specific goal

Farfetched goals such as obtaining as many houses as possible, or for as long as you are wealthy, are very difficult for you to achieve because you cannot define how much is enough. Setting farfetched goals is like trying to piece together a puzzle without having the finished image, or like driving around in thick, heavy fog. Instead of setting unclear goals, let's have specific goals such as: owning 10 houses without having to be in debt. The goal is not 9 or 11; however, it is specifically 10 houses. Whether 9, 10, or 11 is the correct number is not the important issue here. *The strong will and enthusiasm stemming from the concise goals is the important point.* Being specific is like having a compass on a boat; it will help direct you in the right path, even in the midst of a storm.

Goals should be plausible and manageable

When you say, "I want to earn a lot of money" or "I want to own numerous profitable properties", you will find it almost impossible to achieve those goals, as you cannot measure how much is "a lot" and whether you have reached your goal or not. Instead, setting goals such as: "I want to be able to have $1,000,000 within the next 5 years" or "I want to own 10 houses, each with a value of $300,000, within the next 10 years", then you immediately have a goal to work towards.

Many people are not able to achieve their goal simply because they have not *established measureable goals*. Having a specific goal that is clear and concise allows you to know *exactly where you should place your focus*.

Achievable goals should be practical

Talking about achievable goals does not mean that you need to restrict the extent of your dreams to something subpar; in fact, you should dream big for the future. However, you need to divide your goals into smaller goals so that they can eventually become reality.

Example: you are currently unemployed and just took your first step towards real estate investment. You dream of owning 10 houses without being in any debt. You should not set your goal of possessing 10 houses completely debt free within a month or a year. Instead, you should set your goal of owning 1 house first, which is a reasonable goal that is within your reach. After you have achieved that first goal, you continue to increase the standards of your goal *until you reach your ultimate goal* – owning 10 houses and being completely debt-free.

Set a specific timeframe

Only when you set a specific timeframe for your goal you can execute an action plan and feel the sense of urgency in achieving your goals. We do not believe that you need to emphasize an exact date, such as December 31st, 2020. However, having an exact timeframe can help you tremendously. For example, you want to own 10 houses, without being in debt at all, within five or ten years. That timeframe will be a great help to you. Every month and year, you are able to know how your plan is progressing, and the timeframe will help motivate you to achieve your goals.

STEP 4:
Choose the method of earning money in real estate investment

There are hundreds of ways to earn money in real estate investment; however, you do not need to know all of them. You just need to choose one method and master it, and become a professional in the area that you have chosen.

Similar to a car race, you do not need to maneuver all the cars at once in a race; you just need to drive one car and learn to skillfully maneuver it. This will eventually lead you to your victory.

No one becomes a millionaire when they do not know how to choose the right strategy in the "correct" environment.

We have saved the next chapter to specifically address the methods to earning money that are commonly used. You should choose a series of areas that you care about and, after you have finished reading the book and learned the principles, you will then narrow down your focus to just one method.

STEP 5:

Action plan – Determine the tasks that need to be done

When you confirm the tasks that need to be done, write them down and come up with an action plan, which will help transform your dreams into reality. *This is a very important step to get you started and help draw out the specific steps that you need to perform.*

This is Ryan B.'s action plan for his goal of owning two houses within two years:

1. Buy a house before June 1st, 1993.
2. Repair and rent out the house before October 1st, 1993.
3. Increase the rent and sell it by November 1st, 1994.
4. Buy a four-plex before January 1st, 1995.
5. Repair and ask the bank for mortgage before January 4th, 1995.
6. Use the profits to buy 2 more apartment complexes before June 1st, 1995.

STEP 6:

The strategy of backing out and having an emergency plan

Having many strategies of backing out is one of the most important components of your business plan, especially for those who are new to the investment field.

- What will you do in order to back out of an investment?
- What is your emergency plan?
- Will you rent it out to keep it or to sell it after?

What other techniques do you have for stopping the investments preventing loss or a bankruptcy?

You need to find out and clearly confirm what to do before you buy a property.

The last bit of information that you need to remember is that a business plan is a map for directions; however, it is not a law to restrict you. *The agenda provides you with a certain path complete with directions on how to get there.* If you can come up with a plan to keep you on the right track at an appropriate speed, it will help prevent you from stumbling across obstacles on the way. You may encounter some hindrances; however, if you strictly follow your map, you will be able to overcome those obstacles and reach your destination.

You can write out a complicated business plan if you feel that it is necessary; however, you do not need to. A simple investment plan will suffice, as long as it is clear, meets your needs, and has a destination and strategies to get there in a timely manner.

The plan should answer the following questions: Who, What, When, Where, and Why? These questions will help narrow your destination so your plan can be executed more precisely.

KEY POINTS TO A SUCCESSFUL PLAN

1. Be patient

In life, nothing ever goes as planned. There are always obstacles along the way. However, if you have a set goal in mind, patience will lead you to success. For example, when you set out to drive to reach a destination far away, you might be faced with harsh weather or accidents that can affect your path. However, if you have the patience to continue, you will eventually reach your destination. You cannot turn back to where you started just because you hit some roadblocks along the way. Do not let the obstacles stand in your way of achieving your goal. In reality, many amateur investors have *turned back when faced with certain setbacks,* and never actually reached their goal. Investing in real estate is not always a bed of roses. There are always hindrances and obstacles that you need to weather through, and that is the inevitable reality.

Do not give up when you have not achieved your goal. You need to believe in yourself, so that you can overcome the hardships and patiently conquer those obstacles to reach your goal. In the end, you will be fully compensated for all your hard work.

2. Always manage your progress

Manage your progress by checking your plan to see where you are every week, month, and year.

Sometimes, we are so comfortable and are absorbed in just looking far away when driving that we can take a wrong turn that is initially not in our plans. Once we realize that we have made the mistake, it might be too late. It is the same when investing in real estate; if you do not manage and follow up on your progress every week and month, you can easily derail from what your plans are.

3. Be practical

You cannot use a car and expect to arrive on the moon in three days.

Your plans have to be reasonable and practical with your ability, in order to achieve the anticipated goal in a certain timeframe. Plans that are too unrealistic or impractical will lead you to become very unmotivated. However, this does not mean that you cannot be ambitious with your goals. In fact, you should be ambitious, but you need to take time and start out small. Gradually, obtain the small goals that you have set out for yourself. By doing so, you can garner lots of experience and knowledge along the way in order to pave the way towards a much grander plan for the future. This method can help in building your confidence, sense of security, and can easily navigate you to your ultimate goal one day.

For instance, if you only have $1000, you cannot draw up a plan to have 1 billion dollars. Instead, you formulate a plan to earn 1 million, 2 million, 100 million, and gradually with the confidence that you have from the initial success, later successes will become much easier.

Chapter 6
Complete Understanding of the
Cycle of the Economy to Ensure Success

When we first started in real estate investment, we had no clear concept or understanding about this field. As immigrants who had only been in the U.S. for a couple of years and only once witnessed the time period when the price of real estate plummeted in 2000, the words "evolve" or "cycle of market" were completely foreign to us.

The first time we heard those terms was when we visited our teacher, a person with a very generous heart. At the time, he was looking into a decent property near the beach. After thoroughly examining the property, he talked to his real estate agent and asked him to make an offer on the property for 20% lower than the market price.

The real estate agent frowned and replied, "They won't sell it at that price." Our teacher then told the real estate agent: "If they won't sell then I will move on and find another property."

At the time, we were puzzled and asked, "Why did you let go of such a decent property?"

He responded: "The property was decent, but this is during a bad time of the cycle. If the income flowing in was a bit higher, I would definitely take it. However, the flow of income was too low so I decided to not take the offer."

We inquired for more information. "What is the cycle of the market?"

He laughed and said, "The cycle of the market is the process of the market increasing or decreasing."

He saw the confused looks on our faces. He scanned the room and pointed to the clock on the wall and thoroughly explained so we could understand. "Do you see the hand on the clock? The hand moved from 12 and went through all the numbers and came back to 12 as it completed one cycle. It is similar to the night and day: the sun rising and setting would complete one cycle. If you pay attention, you will notice that many events do occur through such a perfect cycle. Real estate properties are no exception; nothing will increase indefinitely and nothing will keep decreasing forever. Once the market is on the rise and falls down to the starting point, one cycle has completed.

"What is the benefit of knowing the cycle of the market?" we continued to ask.

He looked at me and chuckled. "For example, if the 12 on the clock is the peak and the 6 is the bottom of the pit, if you buy real estate properties at the lowest point and sell them at its peak, what will happen?"

"You will get rich very quickly!" I, Khoa, swiftly responded.

"Moreover," he continued, "**knowing the cycle of the market can help the investor preserve capital, to prepare an appropriate strategy to purchase properties at any volatile markets or to back down when necessary.**"

Afterwards, he thoroughly explained what to do when the market is at its peak and when it is at its lowest point. He also gave us the pros and cons of buying properties at the peak time of the market.

The more we listened to him explain, the more interested we were in the subject, once we were able to fully understand how simple it was to garner large profits in investments. Now, we understand the reason why he was always successful in the past 30 years in real estate investment. A great joy that came out of this lesson for us was that we were able to discover another secret of generating money from one of the accomplished real estate investors, *who have mastered the movement of the economy.*

When the market is rising, people who are not knowledgeable are elated with their success or are excited to buy more materialistic assets. In contrast, professional investors just sit back and come up with a plan to buy more real estate properties that they know for sure will be selling at any price when the market starts to decline.

When the market is on the downfall, people who do not have a grasp of the market hesitate, take their time to lament on the situation, and wait for the market to rise again so they can sell the properties.

Meanwhile, when professional investors see any changes to the market, they immediately look for ways to unload the properties that are high-priced and do not bring in good income. They know that, once the market is on the downfall, it will go down at an extremely fast rate, just like a heavy rock on top of a mountain that is falling down to the ground at a rapid pace; no one will be able to stop it. It could be possible that the rock will temporarily stop if it gets stuck between some trees along the mountains; however, the rock will eventually roll down the mountain over time. So when the economy is in crisis, it will take years before the price of real estate can recover to its original state.

It just crossed our minds that if we could get a grasp of the exact time when the market rises or falls, we could buy properties during the period when it is at its lowest and sell at its peak in the cycle, which could bring in huge profits. Just thinking of that made us become very interested, so we asked, "So can you actually know the exact timing of the real estate cycle?"

Our teacher laughed and responded, "No one can know the exact time of the cycle. If they do, the capitalists would have controlled this economy already."

Homer Hoyt, a real estate economist in the 1930s, analyzed the real estate bubble throughout the history of the U.S., and what he found suggested that the bubble occurred approximately once every 18 years. These numbers were accurate until 1925 and, during the period from 1973-1979, there was a huge shift to this cycle.

"However, the main component is not necessarily about having the correct time frame; the important part is to grasp the characteristics, the signals, and the significant points. From there, we can predict the upcoming cycle," he said.

These signs to judge the future market were developed by professional investors, based on their many years of market observation. They have condensed these signs to the following main characteristics of each stage in the cycle:

THE MAIN CHARACTERISTICS OF EACH STAGE IN THE CYCLE

According to Fred Emanuel Foldvary, Ph.D, real estate or any other cycles in the market have their own strong points and go through four similar stages: up, to the peak, down, and back in a circle again.

For the real estate market, the four stages of the cycle are known as: start of boom, end of boom, start of bust, and end of bust. Each stage is recognized through its characteristics, which are listed below.

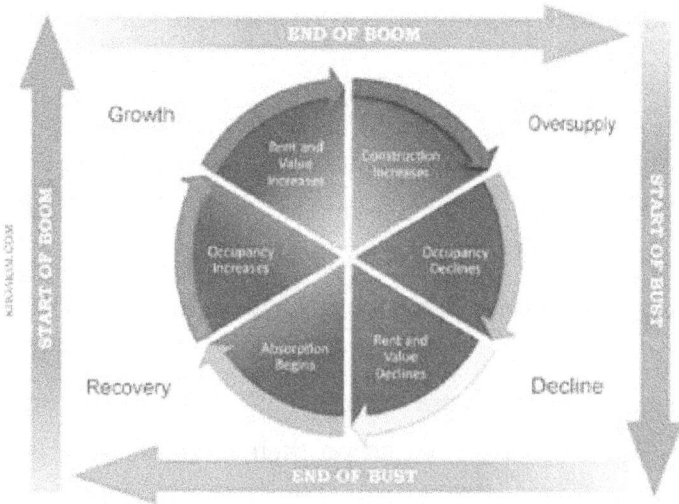

The following list surmises the main points of each stage in the cycle.

A) Start Of Boom

The main characteristics of this period are:
-Low interest, easy access to loans
-Construction of and repair of public highways and bridges
-Rise in the economy
-Rise in jobs, decrease in unemployment
-High demand of properties for rent and an increase in housing
-Increase in the value of real estate properties

The initial step for this increase is mainly due to the government and banks generously decreasing the interest rates to artificially low levels in order to encourage investors and anyone who borrows money to purchase properties.

The notion of expanding and constructing the roads and repairing the bridges triggers an increase in jobs. It helps to decrease the unemployment rate and, when the roads are being constructed or repaired, it starts to open up other opportunities for other sectors, such as cement and steel industries.

Along with the government expanding its notion of providing long-term loans for those companies, there will also be an employment rise. Due to this great progress, the demand for renting or purchasing real estate will also increase. Thus, employees making enough money will lead to high sales in all branches of businesses. Due to the expansion of production, many properties and spaces are being rented out, and this will lead to a shortage of goods. *The shortage of goods will eventually lead to an increase in the price of rent and real estate.*

That shortage will trigger the construction companies to build more new houses, which will lead to an increase in jobs, and eventually will lead to a rise in the economy. This will cause *a dramatic increase in the price of real estate.*

B) End Of Boom

The main characteristics of this period are:
-The quantity of real estate that is being bought and sold is high.
-Many investors plunge themselves into this field.
-Many new houses are being built.
-Increase in rent price
-Increase in the price of real estate
-Many banks decrease the notion of expanding the currency and a decrease in loans.
-Increase in the interest rate

This is the period of time where the price of real estate is at its peak. The price continues to increase at a slower pace. Due to the increase in the rent price, there is high interest on homes, and many do not have the ability to purchase due to their incomes not expanding at the same rate as the real estate on the market. Therefore, many people who purchase real estate during this period of time utilize the programs offered by the government or programs that allow low down payments to qualify for purchasing houses. Another downturn during this period of time is due to the numerous houses that are being built. *This causes a surplus in the market.*

C) Begin Of Bust

The main characteristics of this period are:

-The housing price remains unchanged

-More sellers than buyers

-The price gradually declines

-Increase in unemployment rate

-Increase in the number of foreclosing houses

-The number of real estate properties outweighs the demand for them.

-Many people buy houses using loan programs provided by the government or using low deposit rates.

The beginning of this stage is also called the downfall period. Many banks do not want to loan their money out. They have high interest rates and have many strict requirements for those who want to borrow. Due to there being more sellers than buyers, the quantity outweighs the demands. Therefore, the price gradually declines.

Due to unemployment, everyone will try to cut back their expenses, move back in with family members, or rent at other places that are cheaper. These components lead to a decrease in tax and an increase in vacant homes. In addition, due to the rise in unemployment, people who do not have an income do not have the ability to cover the high monthly expenses. This leads to the increase in foreclosed homes. A number of houses are being sold at any price due to fear.

D) End Of Bust

The main characteristics of this period are:
-There is an increase in surplus of real estate properties.
-Increase in foreclosed homes
-Slow businesses
-Production companies closing down their factories

During this period, the price of real estate starts to hit its lowest point. Many people continue to sell as fast as they can, regardless of the price, because they believe that the price of housing will continue to decrease, Therefore the properties inventory increased, leading to the house prices falling unreasonably or lower than the true value. Then, *the demands for real estate begin to return and prepare for the recovery period.*

If you have a grasp of the main points, from there you can more easily predict the cycle of the market and know whether it is increasing or decreasing. It's like you have a crystal ball that allows you to predict the future. With this knowledge, money-making is just a matter of time.

Now, you have obtained the secrets to being successful from various accomplished investors. We will go to the next step, which is how to establish a career with your empty hands.

PART III
BUILDING AN EMPIRE FROM SCRATCH

Chapter 7
Ways to Build an Empire
Without Having Any Initial Funding

Whether you have a car or a real estate property or nothing at all for a down payment when you request a loan, you can still get started on real estate investment. If you do not have enough funds or any ways of borrowing money, these methods can help compensate for those obstacles and can achieve good results.

Once your system of investment is starting to take shape and has yielded good results as expected, then all the funds will come to you naturally.

First, we will give an overview of these basic methods, then we will discuss them more thoroughly as this chapter progresses. Please remember that you can plunge yourself in to this field at any time that you feel best suits you in regard to your current situation.

- *First, start with no initial funds and not even having the ability to take out loans.*

- *Second, use money from some other sources that is not yours to invest.*
- *Third, apply the skills that you learn to start with just a small amount of capital or resources from others.*
- *Fourth, significantly increase your fortune by investing the profits that you have garnered from initial investments.*
- *Finally, repeat your success time and time again in order to continuously develop and expand your fortune.*

Level one:
STARTING WITH NO INITIAL FUNDS AND BEING UNABLE TO TAKE OUT LOANS

A majority of successful investors nowadays actually started out with no money and were not able to take out loans, but they were still able to succeed through the following methods:

- *First,* Use time and skills wisely in exchange for the lack of funding
- *Second,* Establish capital while simultaneously working and learning the essential strategies
- *Third,* Gain the financial support of people you collaborate with

USE TIME AND SKILLS IN EXCHANGE FOR FUNDING

An Indian immigrant, Haris, came to the United States in 1989 empty-handed. In the early years of settling in this new country, he was working as an IT for a real estate company in Palo Alto. After work hours, he would drive around the city in search of properties that were old, damaged, or burned down. He then contacted the owners of those properties to find out whether they were willing to sell or not. After having thoroughly chatted with the owners, and they agreed to sell the properties, and Haris would immediately assign the contract to other investors in order to rake in profits.

So from then on, Haris had established a routine; he would go to work normally during the day, and he would drive around the city after work hours and on the weekends in search of real estate properties. He would then make appointments with potential investors to assign the property contracts that he had signed. After a period of time, Haris was able to save up some money, and he has used it for investments up until today. In 2008, Haris's assets consisted of five gas stations with a convenience store in each. His monthly income was $60K, which was more than enough for Haris to live comfortably without having to work again.

As you can see, Haris was able to firmly establish his empire just from investing his time in the beginning phase. You are no exception, as you can also start out this way!

ESTABLISHING FUNDS BY SIMULTANEOUSLY WORKING AND LEARNING

The proverbial saying, "killing two birds with one stone", can precisely describe the beginning stages of this career when you initially have nothing in hand. By simultaneously working and learning, this method can help you in garnering *both income and experience.*

The best places you can gain knowledge are real estate or property investment companies. Besides the money that you earn while working, which is essential for investment, you can also gain invaluable knowledge about those fields in the process. Chinese people we know usually utilize this method. When I (Kim) was still in Vietnam, during summer breaks, I would work in order to generate some income. One summer, I found work at an instant noodle company in Cho Lon (a province in Vietnam). After a month of working, during every lunch break, I noticed a young lady around my age who seldom talked and usually sat in the corner in the office after lunch break. Since we were around the same age, I found the courage to befriend her and found out her name was Chieu. She was in the 9th grade, as I was, and our schools were not too far from each other. From then on, we became great friends.

After a long period of time of being friends, I was invited to her house and was amazed at how wealthy her family was. Chieu's father was Chinese and specialized in manufacturing dried food and distributing it to companies all over the southwest region of Vietnam. Every day at that time, her house would have roughly a hundred workers coming in and out, along with about ten trucks to transport the products.

I was very surprised and asked: "Your family is very well-off and has to hire lots of people to help with the workload; why do you have to go out and work to earn money?"

Chieu replied, "My father said that was the best way to learn." At that time, I actually felt sorry for Chieu because, even though her family was very wealthy, she was not able to enjoy and live comfortably due to her parents being stingy. They made her go out and do hard labor even though money was the least of their worries.

However, when I was 20 years old and had just graduated, while our friends were nervously scouting for jobs, Chieu had already accumulated enough experience to manage and run two manufacturing companies for dried foods and one transporting company. It was only then that I greatly admired Chieu's father's vision of "killing two birds with one stone."

The accumulation of knowledge and experience is of great importance for those who are new to this field. You can choose this method to earn an income and also garner invaluable experience in the process, which can be of great help when you officially start to invest in the near future.

Level Two:
USE SOMEONE ELSE'S FUNDS
TO START YOUR CAREER

Sooner or later, but preferably sooner rather than later, you will have to utilize funds from others in order to help develop your investment. Also, you will continuously need to use funds from other investors during the whole duration of your investment.

This method can help you achieve great success even when you only have several hundred dollars. In addition, it can bring you even greater success once you have accumulated your fortune, which in turn can help you leap even further in your investment career.

You may wonder, how can I have enough money for a down-payment while I am unable to get a loan?

You can use the above method or borrow from relatives a sum of money to start your investment. Also, you can collaborate with your relatives or have the financial support of someone in order to get the investment process started.

This is the method William Homes used in order to jumpstart his career. He borrowed $10K from his father and, within a few years, he was able to develop an empire worth $10M.

If you can borrow a small amount of money from friends, relatives, student loans, or credit cards to cover the initial fees, then the rest of the money you need can come from the bank or government-run companies that specialize in helping first-time home buyers. These companies can loan you money with very reasonable rates, and you fortunately do not need a lot of money for a down-payment. This way, you can have complete possession of the property and also reap in lots of profits.

We have a friend named Tony who used this strategy when he graduated from school and had been in the workforce for only one year.

In 2003, Tony bought his first house in Merced, California with a down-payment of $5,000 taken out from *his credit cards.*

As for the remaining 97% of the amount, Tony borrowed it from an assistance program run by the government – a program that supports first-time homeowners. Fortunately, Tony bought his first property right before the real estate market price was skyrocketing; therefore, after about two years in 2005, Tony's property investment had increased to $100K, which he took out to open a small restaurant.

Even though Tony's future investment conquests were not as successful, and he stumbled upon some obstacles shortly thereafter, his story has shown us that you can easily rely on other people's funds as a way to jumpstart your investment.

The following list has some of the assistance programs that help first-time home buyers. You can find more information about them to see which one suits your situation.

Special assistance programs that provide loans to first-time buyers

The fastest way to borrow money is to ask those around you, such as your relatives or friends. These outlets are more accessible because they know you well as a person.

However, if you are unable to borrow money from those you know to fulfill the down-payment, it is not a problem. The following are several outlets that can assist you in loaning the amount that you need for your first step in investment.

- Assistance program to buy a house run by the local government
- Loans provided by the Department of Veterans Affairs
- Assistance program for teachers
- Loans from Rural Housing Service (RHS)
- Federal Housing Agency (FHA)

Assistance program to buy a house run by the local government

You should contact your local government to request someone who can assist you with information regarding this program that helps first-time home buyers.

This program will be managed by the federal government, state government, and local government of where you reside. Annually, this program in the U.S. can allocate up to $200M in assisting first-time home buyers, low-income families, or those who *can manage to buy a house but do not have the funds for a down-payment.*

This program can loan you from $15,000 to $65,000, depending on the county and state of your residence. Even though there is a limit to the amount they can loan you and the assistance can suddenly end, you do not have to worry because this program gets supplemented at the beginning of each year.

You can find out more about this program through the following website:
www.hud.gov/offices/cpd/affordablehousing/programs/home/a ddi/index.cfm

Loans provided by the Department Of Veterans Affairs

If you are currently active or on reserve duty, a veteran, or are widow of a veteran, you can consult the "VA Loan" program. This program allows military personnel to loan up to 103.15% compared to the selling price or value of the house.

This is a wonderful program for those who are qualified. Not only does this program not require you to make a down-payment, but it also does not require you to pay the Principal Insurance Mortgage (PMI) because all the fees will be covered by the government.

You can find out more about this program through the following website:
http://www.benefits.va.gov/homeloans/

Assistance program for teachers

If you are a full-time employee at K-12 public or private schools that are certified by the government, then you are eligible for this program.

Housing and Urban Development (HUD) designed this program to encourage teachers to be homeowners. In order to be considered for this program, *you have to be a full-time employee at a certified school.*

You do not necessarily have to be a first-time buyer in order to participate in this program. However, you cannot be in possession of any other properties at the time, and you must agree to make it your permanent residence for the next three years.

You can find out more information about this program at the following website:
www.fhainfo.com /teachernextdoor.htm

Loans from Rural Housing Service (RHS)

This program provides assistance to those who have low income and those in rural areas of the nation. If you are working in the agricultural industry or if you are living in one of the rural areas, you should ask the bank about this type of home loan to see if you are eligible.

The Rural Housing Service (RHS) program provides opportunities for people living in rural areas to become homeowners, along with programs that assist in upgrading or repairing homes. In addition to having loans available to residents of rural areas, the RHS program also provides loans to the elderly, handicapped, and low-income families.

Federal Housing Agency (FHA)

The Federal Housing Agency is a program that can assist *anyone who is a first-time buyer* and is lacking the funds for a down-payment. This program allows first-time buyers to pay the lowest possible deposit of 3.5% - with a good interest rate, and it does not require you to have a good credit score. That is the best part about this program that sets it apart from the traditional banks.

In contrast, its weak point is that, if your down-payment is low, you have to pay a high Principal Insurance Mortgage, and all the initial fees can increase.

http://hud.gov/offices/hsg/sfh/hcc/hcs.cfm

What happens if you do not have a credit score?

In order to borrow money from the bank, it is necessary to have a credit score. But what can you do if you don't have a credit score?

If you do not have a credit score, you can get in contact with a credit union in your local area. Lots of trade unions recognize the fact that a bad credit score does not equate to an individual with a bad reputation.

Private Loan Companies

If you urgently need money for a down-payment, you can find more information about it through private loan companies such as: hard money and private lender. You can easily search up "private lender" or "hard money" on the internet and you will be presented with a list of websites to choose from. However, you need to be aware that these companies will charge you a very high interest rate. You need to *take extra precaution and thoroughly calculate everything before utilizing one of these private loan companies,* and should only use them if you find great investment opportunities and cannot get loans from anywhere else.

Level Three:
FIND SOMEONE TO COLLABORATE WITH

Many real estate investors have at least worked with someone else when they first started out in this field. Even though these collaborations do not last forever, they are the best way to raise the initial funds needed.

If you happen to find someone who has good properties and benefits, you should find someone to collaborate with and shell out 100% of the investment, while you compose an investment plan and put your knowledge and skills to work.

Where Can I Find These People to Collaborate With?

People who you can collaborate with consist of experienced investors and those who are wealthy and looking for investment opportunities. If you can formulate an investment plan with great ideas that can profit more than 10%, then we are certain you can find very eager investors to collaborate with.

Another option is to collaborate with those who are close to you. They can assist with the essential funds while you handle the repair and maintenance portion.

When a series of banks closed down, a finance employee, Danny, was no exception to the situation. He was also among one of those employees who was put out of work. Being unemployed and living on unemployment benefits had made him restless. Putting his experience as a banker to good use, he found an investment opportunity from a divorced couple who were looking to sell their house. The house was being sold for $200,000. Danny needed $20,000 for a down-payment. However, he did not have enough money, so he asked people close to him for help. Still, he was only able to borrow $5,000 from his father. Therefore, he was left with only one choice, which was to contact someone to collaborate with. After discussing this with his father and a friend, who agreed to contribute the remaining $15,000 for the down-payment along with the repair fees, Danny bought the property and managed the essential repairs and upgrades.

After a couple of months, he sold the property and made a profit of more than $9,000 from this investment.

Even though the amount earned from the investment was not too significant, the ability to earn that much money within a period of two months was not bad at all. In fact, it was more than his usual salary as a banker.

Level Four:
APPLICATION OF THE GRAND METHOD

When you first start out, no matter how big or small your plan is, you must never forget your ultimate goal. That ultimate goal is to build an empire. Unlike other small investors, you cannot stop after a few small successes, as your first steps are only a small part of a much grander plan. With every step that you take, you need to take into consideration the effects that they will have on the development and expansion of your empire. In the beginning stages, you can collaborate with one or two other people to buy several properties and fix them up yourselves. Through this method, you can increase the value of your properties simply by repainting the house after coming home from work or repairing any damages in your free time. After a certain point, you do not need to collaborate with just a few people, but you can work with a larger group in order to generate the utmost profits and simultaneously expand the value of the investment that you have set out to achieve.

When you have the ability to expand or exponentially increase your value by taking advantage of the teamwork and cooperation, you have achieved the ultimate goal.

Just as in the example above, if you can profit $9,000 from each property, why don't you want to increase that number to 5 or

10 properties all at once? Just like that, the amount that you can earn has increased by five, ten, or even more times.

Chapter 8
Ways to Earn Money
From Real Estate Investments

There are numerous ways to earn money in real estate investment, depending on whether you want to invest long-term or short-term in order to choose the appropriate method for your situation.

Normally, many people choose either the long-term or short-term method of investments, and thus they only choose one or two ways of making money. We personally like choose both methods of investments to work hand in hand with each other. Thus, we use many ways of generating money all at once. You can also do that; however, it is very important that you have a thorough understanding and are a professional in each of the ways that you choose.

In order to make it easy for you to follow, we will share these ways of generating money depending on the different strategies.

METHODS OF EARNING MONEY IN SHORT-TERM

Short-term investment consists of the following ways to generate money.

- Buy, repair, and sell immediately
- Wholesaling of real estate
- Assignments of contract
- Real estate referrals

SHORT-TERM INVESTMENT 1:
PURCHASE AND REPAIR TO SELL IMMEDIATELY

Buying a property, fixing it up, and selling it immediately thereafter is the best strategy for newcomers to the field of real estate to reap profits in a short period of time.

You can purchase a property, upgrade, and repaint it before listing so that you can garner some profits right away. It's a great way to start earning money!

Amazing, isn't it?

However, as easy as it sounds, to be successful in this strategy, the investor not only must know how to determine the value and be familiar with the methods to optimize the profits of the property, but he also needs to have a good grasp of the following principles:

Principle #1: Buy under 70% of the market price

When you plan to sell a property at a price of $100,000, then you only want to buy it at a price of $70,000 or lower.

So why is it 70% and not 60% or 80%?

If you are able to buy at 60% or less of the market price, that is a phenomenal prospect that will guarantee to bring you profits for that piece of property.

But there is a catch. You will need to search high and low in order to find properties that are still available and that will be the most profitable.

On the other hand, if you choose to buy at 80% of the market price, you will need to be really frugal when upgrading the property in order to garner even a small amount of profit, or even risk the chance of losing money in the process.

As you may already know, the following are fees that you need to pay out when you purchase a property:

- Commission fees: 4% to 6%
- Title and escrow fees: 0.5% to 2%

- Tax, insurance, and other miscellaneous fees: approximately 0.5% to 2%
- Fees to fix/upgrade the property: 5% to 20%
- Total cost from 10% to 28%

The amount that you need to pay out in order to fix and upgrade the property is always an unpredictable number; it can be 5%, 10%, or even 50%.

If that amount is less that 5%, then you can obtain some profits. However, if you need to pay out more than what you have expected, or the market price has decreased, you will be on the losing end, or you will need to keep that property and wait for the market price to recover.

Principle # 2: Speed

Buy a property in order to fix it and then sell it immediately. The key to success here is the speed at which this occurs. If you buy and sell it as fast as you can, then you can avoid having to pay the following fees:

- Property tax
- Interest
- Utility fees
- Maintenance fees, etc.

These fees can add up and cut a portion of what you are expected to profit the longer you keep the property.

Moreover, the value of a real estate property usually fluctuates in a period of six months. After every six months, the value can increase or decrease. The value of the property will not be the same as what you have initially anticipated; it can skyrocket, but it can also decrease dramatically. Such an incident can rattle your plans, which *can affect the expected profit that you have initially planned for.*

Short-Term Investment 2:
WHOLESALING OF REAL ESTATE

What does it mean to wholesale real estate?

Just like any other manufacturers, when they produce products, they cannot just sit there and wait for customers to come and purchase them. They need to reach out to the local distributors to get the products out to the consumers. This is also the reason why there is a need for wholesalers.

The products of real estate are no different than any other products out on the market; they need the help of distributors to get them out to the consumers. However, the difference here is, instead of the manufacturers, the role of the distributors will be handled by the bank or companies holding mortgage debt or the investment company that owns large amounts of properties. The bank or companies that hold mortgage debt cannot directly sell, and they also do not have the time to sell each of the real estate properties to the consumers. Therefore, they need wholesalers to distribute a significant volume of real estate to the retailers.

What is the way to earn money through wholesaling?

Real estate wholesaling is a lot like flipping houses, but it differs in the fact that instead of flipping houses, *they are flipping lists instead.*

Flipper investors are looking to sell real estate in order to garner as much profit as possible, whereas real estate wholesalers just need to gain several thousand dollars on each property, which is a reasonable incentive for them to sell. Their key to accumulating their wealth is through the quantity of the properties they can distribute.

How much money do I need to have in my possession?

"How can I have a significant amount of money in order to purchase all those properties to sell to the retailers?" you may wonder.

That is a big misunderstanding among many who want to get into the wholesaling of the real estate field. The reality is that these *wholesalers do not purchase the real estate*; they just have the list of properties that are on the market and hand them over to the retailers and private investors in order to gain a small profit.

What is the risk to the wholesaler?

If a wholesaler cannot get properties to wholesale to traditional house flippers and real estate investors, then the risk of being a wholesaler is the loss of their time and money spent on marketing.

Short-Term Investment 3:
REAL ESTATE ASSIGNMENTS OF CONTRACT

What is a real estate assignment of contract?

A real estate assignment is a simple way for you to make money off of a property without ever really owning it. What you are actually doing is looking for a property for which the seller agrees for you to do the assignment. A real estate assignment contract just looks like a conventional purchase contract, but a different part is on the contract with just a few extra words added to your name as the buyer. This would look something like this: "Buyer: Ryan B, and/or assigns."

Once a contract is signed by both parties then you can go ahead and flip it, rehab and rent it, or any other strategy that's legal. But, you can also pass it along to someone else for profit.

In the early stages when we did not have the funds to invest, this was our favorite strategy to get started. Every day, we managed to spare some time to diligently search the list of properties on the market and selected 5-10 potential properties. Then we would send out proposals to buy them from the owners of the listed properties. If no one agreed to sell the properties, it was not a problem, as we would just continue to search for another 5-10 potential properties. If the owners agreed to sell, then we immediately drew up a purchase contract. *Then we showed the value in the deal to one or more buyers in our buyer database and took a referral or "bird-dog" fee for bringing the best deal to them.*

Why assignment contract?

Why don't sellers sell directly to the buyer at a higher price than the assignment contract?

There are numerous of reasons why sellers are okay with it: maybe they're wholesale real estate investors who want to sell their properties to retail investors, or flippers are forced to sell their inventories quickly, or the developers / builders need to clear an old phase in order to replace for the next round of building. Or in the undelayable situations such as the needs of moving out to somewhere else or because of the divorces. these people want to sell their properties as quickly as possible for any price.

Is it legal to find people to assign a purchase contract?

It is legal if your name is on the contract and you have profits; then you can do anything you please with your right of the contract, *as long as both parties (the seller and secondary buyer) have knowledge of the transaction.*

It is illegal when your name is not on the contract and the seller hasn't been informed prior to signing what that means.

This whole transaction should have cost you maybe only $1 out of your pocket with no credit. However, you may be taking a risk if you can't find a buyer to take it off your hands. Thus the money for the contract is held in escrow as a true investor would never put more than $1000 down in order to reduce their risk.

Short-Term Investment 4:
REAL ESTATE REFERRALS

Similar to the case where you find someone to assign the purchase contract, this method is less complex in that no contract or deposit is involved. All you need to do is find good real estate properties that are affordable, and propose them to other buyers or investors in order to receive commission fees.

However, you need to remember that *you only receive commission fees from the buyer and not from the seller.* If you receive money from the seller but you do not have any certification/license in real estate, it is illegal.

Many new investors choose to become distributors, real estate wholesalers, or assign purchase contracts in their early stages of learning to invest without having a lot of money saved up. These strategies are not only simple, but they also do not require them to pay fees upfront *because those properties are almost never owned by them. Therefore, they do not have to worry about being in debt, paying for the repairs, having tenants, or any other miscellaneous fees.*

Ways to earn money in long-term investments

If you choose to do long-term investments, there are usually two ways to generate money flow:

- Purchase and keep it to rent out to tenants
- Real estate transition model or real estate development

Long-Term Investment 1:
PURCHASE AND KEEP THE PROPERTY FOR RENT

A Vietnamese proverb, "ants take time to fill their nest" can precisely describe this strategy.

Every day ants patiently and frequently gather their food, and eventually their nest is filled with food.

A real estate investor purchases a property, keeps it around for rent, pulls in rent money in order to pay the bank debt, and gathers money over the years in order to completely pay off that property.

In addition to time, the inflation of the economy over the years will cause the property to significantly increase in value.

This is the easiest and simplest strategy to build your fortune, even though it may seem slow and uninteresting. However, *as most successful investors say, this is the best strategy that they always use.*

Fundamentals in using this strategy:

- Manage your real estate properly; if not, hire someone to efficiently manage it for you
- Have the ability to keep the property even if the economy fluctuates or through a shortage of income
- Prepare some funds that may be needed for sudden repairs
- Follow the 1/100 rule

What is the 1/100 rule?

Successful investors usually have some very simple rules that come from years of experience in the field that can help to simplify the investment process. Also, these rules can assist amateur investors like ourselves in saving meaningful time while plunging into this field.

The simplicity of 1/100 rule is as follows:

1 unit – 100 Dollars

According to successful investors, for every property that you retain for the purpose of renting out, you must have a net profit of at least 100 dollars.

For example, someone buys a single family home for $300,000 with three bedrooms and two bathrooms, and rents it out for approximately $2000/month.

Fees per month for that home:

Interest for the bank:	$1,100
Property tax:	$312
Insurance:	$60
Utilities, water, garbage:	$80
Repairs (*):	$320
Total fees:	$1872

Therefore, the net profit is calculated as follows:

Income per month ($2000) – total fees ($1872) = $128

The net profit is $128, so you have met the requirements for the 100 rule, which signifies that for every rented home, you profit at least $100.

As a newcomer to this field who wants to establish a sense of security, you should use this rule before buying real estate to rent out until you can find a better method to earn profits.

This rule is simple, but very essential because it comes from many years of experience, and it ensures safety for anyone who wants to invest in real estate. If you understand and consistently apply these rules, it will keep you safe and secure in any market. When I did not know about this rule, we would usually buy based on emotion or based on the rule that says buying investments that are 20% to 30% cheaper than the market is safe. So from 2001 to 2005, we used to go around to different builders from state to state to purchase bundles of properties. Most of our bundles at that time were large two-story houses, from 3000 to 5000 SQF, and we also purchased a few small one-story houses.

At that time, we were thinking that everyone (at least in the Bay Area) likes a big, two-story luxury home. But houses like those in the Bay Area cost from $1,500,000 to 2,000,000 while in New Mexico the same house could be purchased for only $380,000 to 400,000. At that time, I bought properties only below $320,000, following the rule of buying 20% cheaper, so I thought we could sell easily and had nothing to worry about.

But over the course of economic depression of 2007-2009, we found that this rule did not offer any security. When the economy froze, we had properties that we could not sell. Instead, we had to keep them to lease, and when this happened we suddenly saw a big problem. Even though the purchase price was cheaper than the market at only $320,000, but the monthly payment was:

Interest for the bank:	$1,453.54
Property Tax:	$330
Insurance:	$60
Utilities:	$80
Repairs:	$200
Total cost:	$2,123.54

While in the New Mexico region, houses rent for only $ 1000- $ 1200 / month. This meant that we had to take $ 800 to $ 1,200 from our pockets every month for each house.

According to the $100 rule, we were totally wrong, but if someone at that time told us about the rule, we would have laughed them off. This was because we would always follow the 20-30% rule, and we thought that there was no reason to worry.

The truth is that the 20-30% rule is good, but not enough. *This is just good for people doing short term investments.* But for doing long-term investments, when you keep the property in the long term, you may find yourself in difficult economic situations where you need more money each month from your own pocket to keep up with your properties. But if you are unemployed and have no income for many years, you will have huge problems.

In short, if you carefully follow these simple rules, even if you are not a professional investor, whether you are focused on the short or long term, it won't matter if the economy is up or down because you will not be affected. And if you buy real estate in accordance with this rule, the price you pay will certainly be cheap, and your investments will be profitable.

Long-Term Investment 2:
TRANSFORMATION MODEL USED OR REAL ESTATE DEVELOPMENT.

Starting with an *empty lot* that has a value of several hundred thousand dollars, *you can build and develop that lot into a housing complex* with hundreds of units and then the newly-transformed property can now be valued at several million dollars or more.

Former *industrial buildings that are rented out as warehouses are now transformed into business centers and shopping plazas.*

These are the transformations that can be done in order to develop real estate properties.

This method assists in increasing your profits by tenfold or even more; however, you need to spend some time to research the situation before using this method. Besides having experience in investing and a full understanding of the economy, it is also essential to know about the building/developing process. In addition, *it is necessary to have a large amount of funds that can help sustain you for a long period of time while you wait for the development or transition to be approved.* If you do not have enough money to last through this period of time, you can easily fall prey to bankruptcy. We will go into further detail about this in the second book in our series.

After you have selected the appropriate savings plan for your situation, now is the time for you to purchase real estate to invest.

Chapter 9
Typical Sources for
Real Estate Investment Properties

In real estate investment, acquiring source is the biggest problem for investors. Unlike other products that are mass produced, owned by a company, and easily exchanged,"real estate products" are "owned by individuals", and they are difficult to exchange in large quantities or for other special reasons "those products" will be brought to the market.

Building or looking for real estate sources often requires great time and effort, but when you become proficient in it, everything will be much easier.

If you want to become a real estate investor, you must always be savvy in looking for clues, so that the power supply is always abundant for your investment. Whether you operate on a large or small scale, it is just a matter of adjusting volume sources to suit your needs. Usually these are the sources that investors often seek.

- Directly inquire
- Inquire through the press
- Search for real estate on the auctioning list of foreclosure homes
- Search for real estate on the MLS database

Directly Inquire

Directly scout by driving through the specific areas in which you are interested in investing in order to seek any potential real estate that meets your requirement. If you like to purchase houses that need repair and sell them immediately thereafter, this is the best method to find what you need. The condition of these houses might stem from some unfortunate events such as: burned during a fire and waiting for the reimbursement from the insurance company, the owners of the property are elderly people and cannot take good care of the property, the owners are from another state and are renting the property out so they do not have the time and opportunity to care for the property, the owners may have been deceased and the will is being straightened out, or the owners are divorced and are waiting for the settlement. There are countless reasons why the houses could be in such poor condition.

These potential houses usually do not have a good appearance due to: damaged roof, cracked walls, or the lawn looks like it has not been tended to for a long time.

You should write down the address and the specific things that you like about each house. After that, you can search for the address of the owners of those houses through government tax websites. Then, you can directly send a letter to owners to inquire whether they are willing to sell the house or not.

Even though this method might seem old-school, it is still being utilized by many professional investors. The advantage of this method is that you can find some houses that are never listed on the market.

In life, there are many opportunities like these around us. Many people have the assets but, due to poor management, old age, or the property being shared among others, they do not share in the responsibility to manage the essential repairs.

Scouting for properties like these is similar to finding a gem in a puddle of mud. This method can help you purchase the property at an inexpensive price and you can also avoid having to compete with other investors because the property is not on the market.

Scouting for Properties in Newspapers/Classified Ads

Another method of scouting for properties that have not been listed on the market is to search for them in your local newspaper or in the classified ads. Some people want to sell their house on their own without having to list it on the MLS database.

You can either search the classified ads online or in the classic form of a newspaper. Remember to look in the properties for sale category that includes advertisements about investment, direct selling of the property, and a list of houses for sale by a real estate company. You can even look in the houses for rent category and find the phone numbers of the owners of those properties that are not in your local area. Ask the owners about the possibility of them selling the house. Houses for rent have higher potential to be sold because the owners might have suddenly inherited the property and are in the process of renting it out temporarily, or owners have just moved out of the house and are renting it out while contemplating the possibility of selling it. Some homeowners might have been tired of having to deal with tenants due to various reasons such as: elders who can no longer properly manage the property, residing far away from the house and being unable to take proper care of it, or the rented property needs substantial repairs.

The situations vary significantly, but the main idea is if you find a house for rent in your area of interest, you should investigate further to see if it fulfills all of your criteria.

Search for Real Estate on Auctioning List of Foreclosed Homes

"Auction Houses". You might have heard someone who has bought their properties from an auction at the courthouse. So, what is this, exactly?

We all know that unfortunate events can strike anytime such as: death, divorce, terminal illness, or unemployment that land people in situations where they are unable to make mortgage payments. Even though it is devastating to the homeowners who have lost their homes, the lenders are also in a tough position since they may take a loss on the loan, depending on the status of the house during the foreclosure process.

Once the foreclosure process begins, the homeowner or the lender will definitely want to the sell the property as fast as they can. Usually, the houses that are foreclosed carry a lower price tag compared to the market price due to the immediate exchange of cash and the fact that there is no guarantee of proprietorship, as well as any damages that the house might have.

You can find these public foreclosed houses and auctioning events at the following locations:

- The Housing and Urban Development (HUD) office
- Veterans Affairs office (VA)
- The Federal Housing Administration. (FHA)
- The Federal Home Loan Mortgage Corporation (FHLMC)
- The Federal National Mortgage Association (FNMA)
- At the Internal Revenue Service (IRS) (Remember to check with your local IRS office)

In addition, you can get access to this list through the county court of the area in which you plan to invest. You can also find a list of the people who have inheritances. A lot of people who have inherited properties are eager to get rid of them. Also, an advantage to these inherited properties is that they usually have very little or no loan payments left.

Searching for real estate through the MLS database

The MLS database has a significant collection of houses available for investment. The only disadvantage about this source is that many other investors also have access to it. Perhaps they are even searching for the same types of houses as you.

As you will notice, the MLS database continuously changes its list as houses are sold and new houses are listed. In addition, the prices and conditions of the houses can alter during the duration of when they are listed. In order to succeed, you need to diligently check the MLS website and be able to act quickly, should a good opportunity arise.

Furthermore, you need to creatively explore the listings on that database in ways that your competitors have not even thought of. Even though some information on the MLS database can readily be used, only real estate agents who are certified, which grants them full access to all the data on the MLS website.

So, you know where to buy real estate for your investments. Now, let's discover one of the most important chapters in this book...exploring the 4 criteria to buying good properties at a low price.

Chapter 10

Four Criteria to Purchase
Great Properties at a Low Price

In this chapter, you will be guided with practical steps that successful investors have used to estimate the value and carefully select real estate with unbeatable prices compared to the true value. These methods will greatly assist you in earning big profits for your real estate. Even though these methods are designed for investors who operate their real estate business in large quantities, you can also apply these same methods when purchasing any property.

The first three criteria will help you estimate the value and select the best property possible. A good property will have these qualities:

- There is an increase in income stemming from the property over time, which leads to an increase in value of the real estate. When your real estate increases, you will profit once you sell it.
- Property can recover and come back even stronger after being bit by the economy.

The fourth criterion gives you ways to determine the real value of the real estate. You only purchase the property when the price is less than its true value, which is how you will earn lots of profits when you put it out on the market. By applying the strategy of buying real estate at unbeatable prices, the chance of you losing money is close to none. This method not only helps lessen the chance of you losing money but it also assists you in reaping large margins of profits.

Criterion #1:
COMPARE THE CLOSEST PARAMETERS

An important step in the process of finding the best investment strategy is to accurately determine the current value of the investment property. Compare the price of your property to the market price of other properties to find out the price that is closely matched to your property. You need to compare the following parameters:

Most recent houses for sale:

You should have a list of at least *ten houses* that will be sold within six months in order to compare the latest information. However, it will be best if the latest information that you can gather is within the last three months.

Houses within the proximity of where you plan to invest:

You should only compare the houses that you plan to invest with the houses within the *proximity of that area.*

Same square footage:

Remember to compare only the houses that are similar in size. You cannot compare a 1,500 sq. ft. house to a 5,000 sq. ft. house. *The comparison gap of the houses should be only +/-500 sq.ft. ; however, the closer they are in area, the better.*

Age of the house:

Usually, houses that were built in the same area have similar structures, conditions, and basic functions. The best age gap of the houses is *+/- 10 years of each other.* Once again, the closer the better.

Style of the house:

When comparing the parameters of the houses, make sure that they have similar number of bedrooms and bathrooms. If there is a discrepancy, then *it would be best if they only vary by 1 bedroom or 1 bathroom.*

Criterion #2:
POTENTIAL TO GROW

Even if an area had a history of having the potential to develop, it does not guarantee that will be the case for the future. If a big company in that area moves away or the area has any issues or bad situations, that can significantly affect the real estate of that area.

In order to lessen the risk of such an encounter and avoid suffering a big loss, you should thoroughly research and have a good grasp of all the necessary information about the local area.

A teacher of ours told us a story about his friend, who really wanted to purchase a hotel inside the airport in Denver. His friend had thoroughly researched the issue and finally settled on buying the hotel, due to its low price and the fact that the hotel was fully booked every month. Shortly thereafter, he discovered that the airport in which the hotel was located would be moved to another location. Fortunately, he was able to cancel the contract in time and was able to escape from suffering a devastating loss due to a business that had lost its potential to develop.

Despite the fact that the hotel had a great history of development and was still a great business at the time, if his friend had failed to receive that crucial piece of information, who knows what could have transpired in regard to the future of that business once the airport was moved?

Whenever you invest in any real estate, the potential for that area to grow is very important. With that being said, there are some exceptions when we cannot prevent unfortunate events from happening, such as the recent coal mine explosion near Pennsylvania. If there are events that we can know ahead of time and are able to avoid, then we should take careful measures to thoroughly research them and find out more about the potential. When you invest in an area with a great potential to grow, you can be certain that the profits and value of that real estate will continue to increase every day.

The potential to grow for each area can come from the following sources:

- The convenience of the area.
- Its transportation accessibility.
- Large population.
- Big companies with lots of work and employees.
- Good weather.
- Annual population increases, stable jobs.
- Lots of industries, and being surrounded by many companies.

Criterion #3:
RETURN ON INVESTMENT IS
GREATER THAN 6% EACH MONTH

Return on Investment (R.O.I.) should always be higher than 6%. The R.O.I. allows you to know how much profit is made compared to the amount of capital spent for the investment.

The R.O.I. is calculated by taking the profit and dividing it by the amount invested. *Profit is the monthly income after all the fees are taken care of, multiplied by twelve and divided by the total amount of money spent on the investment.* R.O.I. is a crucial number that needs to be carefully examined, and is used to estimate the profit of the real estate.

It is very easy to calculate the R.O.I. for a single home or condominium. You just need to find out how much the rent is for the houses in that area that are similar to the houses that you plan to invest in. Then, take the amount of money collected each month, multiply it by 12 months and divide it by the amount of money you spent for the investment, and finally multiply that number by 100.

Example: you purchase a property for $240,000, you pay a down payment of $48,000 (20%), the rent for that area is $2000/month and, after all the fees are counted for, you receive a total of $500/month.

The equation to calculate the R.O.I. will be as follows:

$$[(500 \times 12) / 48{,}000] \times 100 = 12.5\%$$

That is an example for a single home but, if it is the case of an apartment complex or business plaza, a few shady businesses can manipulate their numbers to make them more appealing. Even though occurrences like this rarely happen, they are not unheard of; therefore, you need to be careful in calculating the total amount of income for that property.

Why do we need to know that the R.O.I is 6%?

When you follow the strategy of profit over capital investment that is higher than 6% per year, it will help you feel more secure that your capital investment will achieve decent results. Of course, the R.O.I. can vary on a case-by-case basis; however, that number (R.O.I.) should not be lower than 6% per year. If that number is lower than 6%, it is not worth the time and energy that you put in towards the investment, because you are responsible for paying interest, managing tenants and maintaining the property. If that is the case, you would rather place your money in the bank so you can have a steady profit and not headache.

Criterion #4:
DETERMINE THE TRUE VALUE

Good markets to invest in are the ones that have properties valued at a price lower than their true value. In order to accurately determine the true value, professional investors usually have a very simple way of calculating those numbers. They take the total amount of income generated from the property and divide by its value. If that number is higher than 6%, the property is either equal to or lower than its true value, whereas if the number comes out to be less than 6%, that property is either equal to or higher than its true value.

Just as in the example discussed above, you purchase a property for $240,000 and the monthly rent in that area is $2000.

The equation to calculate its true value is as follows:

$$[(2000 \times 12) / 240,000] \times 100 = 10\%$$

After all the calculations, if the number is less than 6%, it signifies that you purchased the property at the market price, or higher than its true value. If that number is at least 6% or higher, then you have bought the property either at the market price or lower than its true value.

If the price of the real estate is lower than its true value, it is certain that the property will continue to increase to its true value or even higher in the future. This notion depends on whether the economy or the area in which it is located has the potential to grow in the future.

By knowing the true value of the property, you can determine the price at which you want to purchase. This piece of information can assist you in obtaining more profits than other investors. You can safely bid even higher than others to possess an investment and still get a large profit margin.

Knowing the true value can help you determine whether the market price is at its peak so you can decide whether you want to keep or sell the property.

You need to compare the current market price to the true value, even if the property has doubled its value. In addition, you should not sell the property if the market price is less than its true value. You should continue to keep the property around until its price is higher than the current price and also higher than its true value.

So, what happens if the price goes down? How low should the price be before you sell it?

A lot of investors follow the rule of 5% in cutting their losses, which means that, when the real estate falls below 5% of the price at which they purchased, they will sell immediately in order to lessen the loss even further.

With short-term investors, this strategy makes perfect sense. *However, as a long-term investor, you need to look further into the issue and figure out a reason for it.* If it is due to the economy, then it is up to you to decide whether you want to keep or sell the property. If the reason is the fall of the economy, the economy will eventually increase again because the field of real estate always has its cycle of ups and downs. Instead of worrying about the collapse of the economy, you should grasp this opportunity to purchase even more properties, because any collapse will end.

If the profits for the property fall below the secure rate, or there is an increase in expenses needed for repairs, an increase in vacancies, or an inability to manage the properties, you should carefully reevaluate the situation before selling.

In general, you should sell the property only if it falls within these five situations:

- You made a mistake in determining the value area in which the property is located, which violated the two strategies listed above.
- In the midst of receiving the monthly income from property, you realize there are negative changes to the first two strategies mentioned above. Moreover, these negative changes are not momentary. For example, the number of companies in the area has decreased, there are lots of vacant houses unable to attract tenants, there is a high unemployment rate, people are starting to move elsewhere to reside, the weather is bad, etc..
- The area has a high crime rate, and you do not have the ability to manage the property.
- You find a better property compared to the true value, even though the property that you currently possess is already decent. You can sell that property and invest that money to purchase an even better property.
- The property has already exceeded its true value.

PART IV
INCREASE THE CAPITAL INVESTMENT
RAPIDLY AND SECURELY

Chapter 11
Ways to Increase the
Value of Real Estate Investments

When you are able to purchase a property at a low price and at the appropriate time, you have already secured your gain in this field. However, in order to shorten the timeframe to achieve your ultimate goal and to optimize the value of your real estate, it is necessary to know the rules to increase the profits of the real estate.

This is one of the secrets that successful investors have utilized in order to optimize their assets and profits in a rapid manner. Normally, when you invest at the right time, you can profit about 20%, 30%, or 40% per year. However, if you know the clever strategies to increase the value of your assets, you can easily increase your profits by 100%, or even up to 200% with just one slight change .

The best methods to increase the value of real estate are as follows:

- Increase the value by making any necessary repairs.
- Increase the value by increasing the profits.
- Increase the value by altering the applied models.
- Increase the value by fixing any mistakes.

Besides the method that requires you to make some necessary repairs, which might cost you a bit upfront, the remaining methods will help to optimize the value of your real estate without being costly. Not only do these methods not require a lot of spending, they also will assist you in achieving the best results possible. The only requirement is for you to try your best at investing, be patient, and use your imagination to make your ultimate goal a reality.

Increase the Value of Real Estate #1:
MAKE ANY NECESSARY REPAIRS TO INCREASE ITS VALUE

The quickest way to increase the value of your real estate is to simply repair any damages that the property may have or any areas that are not very appealing.

Usually, there are many repairs that can be made to a house; however, repairing everything in the house will be a very costly process. Repairs such as changing the whole underground plumbing system, changing the electrical system, or altering the sheetrock of the walls in the house might not even guarantee an increase in value for the property.

So, which repairs should be made in order to increase the value of the house?

According to experienced investors, when buyers, renters, or banks determine the price of a house, they rely mostly on how appealing the outer appearance is. They usually do not pay attention to, or determine the price based on, very detailed specifications of the house that are not visible. The upside of this notion is that anything that can be seen with the eyes is usually not very costly to repair, compared to the repairs that are not readily visible.

Therefore, you can save money and simultaneously optimize the value of your real estate. Usually, professional investors strongly recommend the following repairs to be done to the house:

Build more bathrooms

Surveys on real estate show that bathrooms have a significant effect on the value of the house. The greater the discrepancy between the number of bedrooms to bathrooms, the greater the demand for additional bathrooms to be added to increase the value of the house. This increase in value far exceeds the amount of money that you need to spend on making that implementation.

Enhance the appearance of the kitchen

The kitchen is another top aspect that has a great significance to the value of the house. However, it is unnecessary to upgrade the whole kitchen into a state-of-the-art masterpiece, or to have imported materials made in Italy. Unless the owner has a passion for cooking, the amount invested to have the kitchen fully upgraded is a waste and will not garner much profit.

Repaint the house

One of the quickest ways to visibly increase the value of the house is to repaint both the inside and outside. A Vietnamese proverbial example of this notion is when a country girl is given the chance to don a beautiful silk blouse. The new paint will have the same effect, as it will help to lighten up and eliminate any old residues of the house. This method will instantly increase the value.

Flooring

The flooring should be clean and modern. Its color should be uniform, and match with the ambiance of your house. Therefore, it is essential to consult with different sources to ensure that you do not choose certain styles or colors that do not appeal to most people.

Windows and doors

Replacing existing windows and doors with modern and sophisticated styles can make your house much more appealing to the public. Even though there are a plethora of styles you can choose from, you should carefully research the houses that are currently being sold on the market to narrow down your choices.

The surroundings and lighting

Invest in making your front/backyards much livelier and interesting with various plants, flowers, and different types of rocks. In addition, pay attention to how your house looks at night.

Increase Real Estate Value #2:
INCREASE THE PROFITS

What exactly is increasing profits and income? This is achieved by *increasing the rent price of your property, which will increase your income.*

Is this possible?

If you rent out your apartment complex for a monthly fee of $800/per unit, then you can increase the rent to $1000/month by enhancing the landscape to make it more appealing adding a playground for children at the apartment complex. With these implementations, you can increase the monthly rent. Will this method actually work?

If your property is rented out as $0.50/sq ft., you increase that number to $1.00/sq ft. Will this help to increase the value of your real estate? The answer is yes!

This is the method that Ron, a successful real estate investor from Santa Clara, California shared. He bought an industrial building that is 100,000 sq ft. with a price of $5 million. He is currently renting that building out at $0.50/sq ft., which will generate $50,000/month in rent. The tenants that he is renting to have only six months left on the contract.

However, Ron does not want to stop there; he thought of ways to increase the value of the real estate instead of persuading the tenants to continue to rent his property, he announced that he will increase the rent price within the next year. If the tenants do not agree to this term, they can choose to move out.

Ron's friends think his strategy for increasing the rent price during the downfall of the economy is irrational. Even with his friends' objections, Ron still persists in following through with his plan.

One day, Ron is chatting with one of his friends, who is looking for a place he can use as for storage, so he can sell wholesale items. His friend is searching high and low for the perfect place because all the properties he has looked at are too big, which will be a waste as he will not need all that extra space.

An idea immediately flashes in Ron's mind; if he rents out the 100,000 sq ft property *to just one industrial company*, then the rent price is probably only be $0.50/sq ft. However, *if he divides the property up into small pieces and lets many small manufacturing companies rent,* operating both as storage and as a place where they can sell their products, this will make it easier for Ron to rent out the property, and at the same time the rent price can be higher than just renting it out to one big company.

So, Ron immediately invites that friend to take a tour of his property, and gives him the choice to rent out as much space as he wants. His friend is elated and wants to rent out a small part of the property at a price of $0.80/sq ft. Ron readily agrees to the deal and even promises his friend that, for every referral he makes to anyone wanting to rent out the property, he will give him six months free of charge.

When the friend mentions to Ron about having another friend that is interested in renting out a small part of the property to use as storage and as a wholesale store, the price to rent out Ron's property is now raised to $1.00/sq ft.

Ron then tries to publicize his building even further through banners and billboards around the city and he convinces many small manufacturers to rent out the space at his building.

After eight months of renting out the whole building, Ron comes to the bank to disclose the amount of income per month. The bank immediately determines the price of the building as no longer $5M; instead the building is now worth over $9M.

To become a successful investor and optimize the initial investment money, you need to always think of *ways to increase the value of your real estate to its fullest.* Once you have raised the value of your property, it signifies that you have increased the income of the property, which also suggests that you have increased the capital of the property. Through this process, you have ultimately increased your overall wealth.

Increase the Value of Your Real Estate #3
ALTERING THE APPLIED MODEL

Usually when people hear of changing the model that is being used, they think of a change in the architectural style, whereby a completely modified model is used in place of the existing model.

You can go that route if you have a carefully planned concept and a clear path of how your business will operate to generate more profits for you than the existing plan. On the other hand, if you do not have a clear direction of where you want your business to head, you should not think about altering the architectural style of the property, as it can be quite expensive to do so.

The act of altering the existing model that the professional investors are talking about can help you dramatically increase the value of your real estate many times; you do not need to spend too much to achieve such goals. This is achieved *by altering the existing model of real estate on official documents.*

What does this mean?

The investors examine the documents and alter the industrial buildings into offices or turn them into individual houses that specialize in caring for the elderly. As for the millionaire investors from the 80's and 90's, they turned apartment complexes that were owned by *only one owner into separate condominiums to sell them to multiple owners.*

This process just requires the use of a lawyer who specializes in this area, or you can request the necessary papers to process this transition at your local government.

Increase the Value of Your Real Estate #4
REPAIR ANY FLAWS IN YOUR REAL ESTATE

What does "repair flaws" entail?

To repair any flaws in your real estate is to *fix any problems associated with your property and turn it into a selling point.*

Robert Kyosaki, the author of numerous books on how to become wealthy, retold the story of when he was taking a stroll on a hill and saw a sign for a house for sale. He approached the house to ask for more information and found out that the house had been on the market list for over two years, but it was still not able to sell. The reason was that the house was situated on top of a hill, thus it required the use of a well for water supply. The source of water in this well had been dried up. Due to that problem, the owner agreed to sell the property to him at a much lower price compared to the market price.

After Robert purchased the property, he promptly asked people to come and dig a different well adjacent to the previous well. With just a few thousand dollars, he was able to efficiently fix the problem. He also repainted the house before putting it on the market. Through the sale of this house, he was able to garner tens of thousands of dollars easily, just by putting in some effort and thought into fixing a small problem that came with the property.

In another story told by Donald Trump, a billionaire who specializes in investing in real estate, he also had to fix up several flaws of a property and, in return, he was able to yield a sizeable amount of profits. That property was 40 Wall Street, an old building that was built in 1920 in the business district of New York. The building was in an ideal location and was owned by the mega investors, and the corporations had spent millions of dollars to invest in this building, but were not successful.

After thorough research, Trump realized that there were problems inside the terms of the leasing contract. The building was built on a rented piece of land, and the leasing contract was outdated and had numerous disadvantages to the owner of the building. This had caused difficulty to everyone who wanted to shell out money to repair and enhance the building or rent it out to others.

Since obtaining the contract for rent was a problem, that problem needed to be fixed. However, the representative of the property owner was adamantly against changing the regulations of the old contract while the owner of the property was in Germany.

Trump decided to fly to Germany to meet with the owner of that property, and he was able to convince the owner to rewrite the contract to lessen the restrictions on repairs, and approve the building to be converted into offices or an apartment complex. In the end, Trump succeeded.

Through this ordeal, he had converted an empty office that he bought for $1M into a successful commercial building valued at over $350M.

Successful real estate investors all agree that **the most important aspect to becoming wealthy in this field is to purchase a building and use various methods to optimize the value of the property. In addition, the altering of existing models can contribute to the**

increase of value for your real estate. These methods will ultimately help you generate lots of money.

So now that you know the most important ways that professional investors increase their investment assets, if you actually apply them seamlessly in your investment, they will certainly bring you tremendous financial progress.

Chapter 12
Principles That Can Ensure
Your Success in Investment

Congratulations on finishing Chapter 12, which signifies that you have made it more than half way through the book. In the last twelve chapters, you have been presented with many effective methods that can readily be used. Before we go on any further in developing an empire of your own, let's outline the fundamental steps utilized by professional investors that have ensured success in the investment field.

DON'T LET EMOTIONS AFFECT YOUR
INVESTMENTS

Real estate investment is of great value, so investors usually have very strong feelings about it when they purchase or sell a property. The seller always wants to garner the utmost profits, so they try to set a price as high as possible. In contrast, from a buyer's perspective, the lower the price, the better it is.

The two parties would want to negotiate with each other, as each party always wants to obtain the most benefits for their side.

Therefore, if you show signs of frustration and discontentment during a negotiation, you risk losing many good deals.

An investor friend of ours, Mike, was notorious for being firm when it comes to negotiating a contract; he would always refuse to negotiate.

On one occasion, after days of negotiating and the deadline for the contract fast approaching, after an appraisal of the property, the buyer saw many problems that needed repair and wanted to negotiate the price again. This prompted Mike to become furious, and he decided to call off the contract completely. Even when the buyer wholeheartedly pleaded with him, he sternly refused to give the buyer another chance to negotiate.

Shortly thereafter, he put that property back on the market for sale. Even though he tried really hard to sell it, the price was far lower than what the first buyer had previously offered. Mike was able to release his frustration at the moment when he sternly refused the first buyer, but he had to pay the hefty price of losing a lot of profit and a period of several months before he could earn back his capital.

Personally, we have also experienced an incident where our feelings have gotten in the way of a business venture. That time, our friend introduced us to a business plaza that was in the process of being built by a big investor who was about to go bankrupt. After agreeing to buy the property and work out all the terms and conditions, the seller made one more request. He stated that if we wanted to continue building the plaza, we would need to use the same workers that had worked for him.

The cost of building that plaza was quite expensive, so we decided to reject that request. After negotiations back and forth, we became frustrated because we just did not want to be bound like that and decided to end the contract. That act had caused us a loss of close to $300,000 in profit. Another buyer purchased that property and sold it immediately without finishing the plaza. Within a short period of time, that buyer was able to reap in close to $300,000 in profit.

Evidently, you cannot obtain any profits if you show signs of frustration or discontentment stemming from the selling/purchasing of a property. If you allow your feelings to get the best of you, you will easily let a once in a lifetime opportunity slip from your grasp.

PATIENCE

Whether you are patiently negotiating a contract you have desired or are patiently waiting for a good opportunity to purchase a property, patience is still the greatest quality that can bring you success in this field.

As you already know, real estate investment always has its cycle of ups and downs. Therefore, as a good investor, you have to be *patient when the market is down in order to make a purchase,* and also being patient when holding on to the property during the period when the market hits rock bottom, until the value increases once again. Even if you can afford it, but you lack the patience when the market is falling miserably and get rid of your property at any price, you have given the professional investors a chance to rake in all the properties that you have discarded. Those properties that you might have worked tirelessly to obtain will now belong to those other patient investors.

Professional investors, even when the housing market is on the rise, can completely disregard what everyone says while they sit back and patiently wait for the opportunity to arise. Waiting like a tiger to strike, once the right moment comes along, pouncing on their prey, they will put their utmost effort in capturing that opportunity.

According to professional investors, patiently waiting for the right moment can actually instantly increase their capital by two or three times. Usually, it takes about 5 to 10 years for the capital to double; *however, investing during the period when the economy is down can easily double one's capital within one to two years.*

Therefore, in order to become a successful real estate investor, patience is a vital quality that you cannot forgo in this learning process.

RESEARCH THE CURRENT ECONOMY

In real estate investment, the economy can undergo similar effects; however, the extent of the increase or decrease of each area depends on the overall development such as: jobs, airports, railroads, migration, expansion of mega companies, and safety issues, which can significantly affect the value of real estate investment.

For example, Detroit, Michigan was once a big industrial city that specialized in manufacturing cars in the United States . Between 1950 and 1980, the population of Detroit was 1.0 million people, and the growth was the third highest in the country. However, due to the mega companies moving elsewhere for their business along with safety being an issue in the area, the population was decreased by 50% by 2013 and the housing market of Detroit plummeted.

Las Vegas and Arizona are other examples of this phenomenon. During 2003-2004, when the building industry was at its peak, many workers came flooding in to find work and reside there. This caused the housing market to skyrocket. However, in 2006-

2007, construction companies decreased their workload, which caused the workers to lose their jobs. Since many people lost their jobs and moved elsewhere to make a living, the real estate in these areas hit rock bottom.

Therefore, it is crucial that you carefully manage the area of your real estate investment so you can predict whether the value of the properties in that area will increase or decrease. *This can determine whether you want to increase your investment money or withdraw from it in time, so as not to lose any capital.*

MAKE MONEY WHEN YOU BUY REAL ESTATE, NOT WHEN YOU SELL IT

As you already know, our financial condition during 2005 was very distressing, partly due to not having a good understanding of this method.

During that time, we possessed many properties around California, Nevada, Arizona, and Florida.

Not mentioning all the other mistakes that we made in investment, such as the lack of careful management of the properties, we are talking about not having a grasp of this very basic method. According to a book of tips on how to become wealthy by Robert Kyosaki, we "counted the number of chickens before the eggs even hatched." Due to that wishful thinking and dreaming of the amount of profits that we could garner, we bought a series of properties at high prices. We "happily" spent money every month to cover our debt, even though our "chickens" had yet to hatch.

The economy then crashed, and the value of real estate plummeted depressingly. Some of the properties we bought at 15% or 20% lower than the market price could withstand for a short period of time, and the rest of the real estate we rushed into buying could not endure in such a dire state of the economy. We had to accept the loss of capital and sell off all those properties at any price in order to survive.

Always remember this method before you decide to purchase real estate. *Do not let your assets and hard work slip away due to some wishful thinking* because, once you have participated in this game of buying properties, it is too late. You need to be reminded that *"you earn money when you buy, not when you sell."*

Chapter 13
Attract Good Fortune in Your Direction

Similar to how a magnet can attract iron filings, you should also attract good fortune to your direction. You should create resources for these fortunes to arrive by exercising the ideas and experiences that you have obtained from previous successful investors. In addition, you can cooperate with others to invest and develop your career into a success.

The following are methods that you can utilize in order to create your own fortune.

Attract Good Fortune 1
FIND SUCCESSFUL PREDECESSORS IN YOUR FIELD
AND LEARN FROM THEM

Clever investors never hesitate to ask for assistance when they need it. They know their limits and fully understand that they need to seek advice from professionals in their field in order to quickly achieve their goals.

You do not assume that you can write your own prescription when you are ill, just as you cannot act as your own lawyer and defend yourself in a complicated court case. Unfortunately, even though many people know when to visit a doctor for medical reasons and rely on the law to protect them, but, when it comes to investments, they suddenly plunge themselves into this field without consulting or learning from the successful predecessors that have years of experience in the field.

We live in a world of information; **whoever has access to the most accurate information will easily achieve success.** In the end, you will be the person with lots of information in the field of your choosing. However, before you get to that step, you need to take full advantage of the experiences and mistakes that the predecessors have stumbled upon to help you avoid those same unfortunate incidents and change for the better.

Attract Good Fortune 2
FORM A GROUP OF PROFESSIONAL REAL ESTATE INVESTORS

It is impossible for one person to know everything, regardless of how smart you are or how much experience you have. Therefore, professional investors recommend that you should learn and cooperate with others in order to form a much stronger unit.

The best recommendation from these investors is to form a group of experts in real estate investment since the real estate field is very dynamic. You are incapable of being an expert in all the different categories of this field. Trying to learn everything yourself might be a bit too far-fetched and will also be a very costly process.

Who are these experts?

- Real estate agents in the area
- Home Inspector
- Lawyers
- Architects
- Residents of that specific area

Talented Real Estate Agents

These are the people who you will have a long-term relationship with who will assist you in selling real estate at a decent price. Real estate agents have knowledge about the economy, skills in negotiating with clients, strategies in setting the price, the ability to calculate tax, and the ability to increase the value of the properties, so they will sell at a higher price than usual.

Home Inspector

Once you have found a potential property, it is easy to let your optimism overlook the repairing fees. Miscalculating the repairing fees – whether it is short or you have left out some repairs that need to be done – will result in smaller amount of profits than you anticipated.

Home Inspector will assist you in having a complete understanding of the repairs that need to be done for that property, which will make it easier for you to visualize and avoid any risks of losing profits when calculating repairing fees.

Consult with lawyers about the law

If you are not very familiar with the procedures, the best solution is to consult with your lawyers or any law personnel. They will help manage the contracts, clauses, and laws concerning the procedures of selling and buying real estate.

Architects

Architects are experts in construction; thus, they can be of great help in inspecting any faulty areas in the house, such as the structure, roof, ceiling, etc. They can also consult with you regarding any upgrades, repairs, or any intricate designs that

174

can increase the value of the house. Clients are always attracted to houses that are immaculate, with a beautiful design, and those that do not require many repairs or can easily be repaired if needed.

Residents of That Specific Area

These residents have a good grasp of the information regarding the housing market, residential complexes, and the key attractions of the area that you invest in. There are times where the residents of the specific area where you plan to purchase a house have even more valuable information than the experts. They can help you save a substantial amount of money.

The advantages of having a group of trusted experts

Advantage #1:

You will learn from other investors' mistakes and the experiences that they have had over the years in this field. These valuable lessons will help you avoid making those same mistakes and effortlessly deal with them should the situation arise.

Advantage #2:

Within the same group, you can garner even more success, faster and easier. You can compensate for each other's weaknesses as a team. In addition, you can console members of your team when they are faced with hardships and, inversely, they can also be the ones to lend you support when you encounter disappointing situations. They can assist in making up for any flawed skills that you may have. As a team, everyone can "run" at a faster pace. A supportive group of four people can run a mile much faster than one person running alone. Hence, if you want to achieve that great pace, you need to work with a group.

Advantage #3:

Each member of the group knows at least 100 valuable contacts. Therefore, a group of six people will have 600 possible contacts. If each of the 600 contacts knows 100 other contacts, then you can actually form relations with 60,000 valuable contacts. However, these numbers are not quite accurate. People have calculated the value of a network is simply the square of the number of people in it. If your network has 600 people, then the ultimate number of valuable contacts you can have is: 600 x 600 = 360,000.

Attract Good Fortune 3
BECOME A STUDENT FOR LIFE

According to the experts, in order to become successful, investors need to continuously research the areas of interest, always consult with other investors about any new information, and attend seminars regarding real estate investment once every few months.

Professional investors who have a long-standing career in the areas that they have chosen are not necessarily more talented than others. However, they are the ones *who know how to take advantage of time in order to learn the essentials and outshine their competitors.*

In order to be well-trained, they have to practice investing every day to obtain valuable experience and have a good grasp of even the smallest details to become an expert in the field. As a result, they will be able to predict and obtain the opportunities that may arise, whereas other investors who are not so suave in this field cannot foresee those valuable opportunities.

This lesson helped us find a favorable opportunity to invest in Nevada many years ago.

It was an apartment complex with 44 units in Northern Las Vegas, where 50% of it was vacant and the bank had an asking price of $1.1M. With that price and the fact that 50% of the units were vacant, the amount of profits per year was approximately 6%. If all the units were occupied and with all the miscellaneous fees taken into consideration, there would be a profit of about 13%, which is a pretty good profit margin for most investors. However, the apartment complex was listed on the market and, even with more than six banks, it was not able to sell.

The problem was that it was built in 1963 and lacked an efficient sewage system. A sewage system needed to be built; however, it would be one that was above the ground and was fully visible by the public. Each month, the owner of the complex needed to pay about $2000 to maintain and clean the sewage system, so it could operate smoothly and without any odors.

For that reason, the complex had a very modest asking price and, even though many interested investors came to take a look, they all decided not to buy it. The complex was sitting on the market for six months and unable to sell, and the bank was eager to take it out.

After researching and realizing that this was an opportunity, we concluded that:

- We would implement a sewage system that connected with the public system, as we noticed there was a hospital and shopping plaza about 500 meters away.
- If that did not work, we would put in a septic tank, which is a sewage system that was similar to the system in Vietnam.

As I, Kim, recall when I was young, when the designated day to clean the toilet came around, I would always run away because I could not stand the deafening sound of machinery and the odors that would eventually diffuse to the whole village. However, every time the truck that cleaned the toilet drove by after it was done, everything returned to its normal state. Almost everyone in Vietnam lived through this type of sewage system as long as they could remember, which seemed perfectly normal to them.

After carefully researching the fees and the potential profits of the different solutions, we sent in an offer to the bank with our own asking price of $760K. After several weeks of back and forth negotiations with the bank, they agreed to sell to us for $820K. After acquiring the property, we built a sewage system at a cost of only $55K. And now, that complex no longer needs maintenance fees, which saves us close to $2000/per month and ultimately increases the total profits per year up to 16%.

Attract Good Fortune 4
EXPERIMENT WITH A SMALL MODEL

Before fully immersing yourself in the ocean, you should first test out the water with your toe, then your leg and then gradually move into it.

Real estate investment is similar to the experience depicted above. Your goal is to develop your business on a large scale; however, you need to start out with small models first before reaching your ultimate goal. Through the small models along the way, you will be able to acquire lots of experience. You will be able to apply the successful methods learned from the first house to invest in the second house, then the third, fourth, and eventually up to a point where you are satisfied with your empire.

Just like Richard constructed his models by buying his first house that was in the proximity of his workplace, so he could better repair and manage the tenants after work hours. Through this process, he was able to learn many repairing skills, along with management skills. In addition, through those experiences, he discovered other ways of increasing the rent and the value of the house, all the while decreasing the managing fees. The experience from the first house led Richard to manage the second house, then on to his third house. Just like that, he was able to accumulate lots of experience over time. He currently manages one hundred properties, and his real estate asset is valued at over $12M.

In Stephanie's case, she was a recent college graduate with salary of a $2500/month as a nurse in training. After working for one year, she bought her first house. Everyone close to her was worried about how she would manage the property in the long run because loans from the bank, taxes, personal expenses had taken up most of her salary. However, Stephanie had a plan: she went to work the whole day and rarely went or cooked at home and she saved the master bedroom to have a separate entry for herself to live, while she rented out the main house to a family with two young children. *The tenants' rent money would be paying her mortgage and utilities*, while she just had to worry about the property tax.

Shortly thereafter, other people were interested in renting the house, so she built a small house in the back lot that was vacant. She then rented that new property out to a small family.

The success from that initial investment had given Stephanie the idea of going into business. She noticed there were a lot of young people her age who were getting their start in the business world but who were unable to make payments for a whole house. But if someone buys a house with two units, lives in one unit and rents the remaining one, this will help them not to worry about the mortgage.

From that idea Stephanie bought small cheap properties on big lots and added more small units behind them to sell. She then went on talk shows and to seminars to share her experiences. Stephanie's plan worked out flawlessly, which prompted her to dedicate all her time to operate this booming business.

You can also test out small models just like the examples above. Through this method, you will realize that the process to managing an empire of your own will be much easier.

Attract Good Fortune 5
PROTECT YOUR FORTUNE

It will be a devastating loss if the assets that you have poured your tears and sweat into have all gone up in smoke, right? It is an unfortunate event, but it can happen to anybody, anytime. Many people become empty-handed overnight due to an accident, an illness, or becoming tangled in a senseless lawsuit. However, *successful investors know how to use lawyers, insurance companies, tax experts, and accountants as their unbreakable barricade.* They try their best to avoid getting tangled in lawsuits that can stem from these countless business deals.

Due to this subject being out of the realm of this book, we recommend that you seek assistance from professionals in each field. These experts can help you take full advantage of the resources to protect your fortune such as through: insurance, credit unions, international bank accounts… and ensure that no one and nothing can harm your hard-earned assets.

Attract Good Fortune 6
MANAGE YOUR ASSETS AND DEBTS

Have you ever heard of some people who got lucky with their first few investment successes and garnered a lot of money but, after a short period of time, were left empty-handed? Or those skilled investors who have a sizeable assets that would be the envy of many, but who suddenly go bankrupt or live in poverty?

Why does this happen?

Many people believe that it is enough to be successful and able to accumulate lots of properties. In contrast, that perception is only a small portion of success. The reason why real estate investors who are able to generate millions of dollars still fall prey to unfortunate events such as facing bankruptcy or living in poverty is due to the lack of effective management of their assets and debts.

Hence, when your real estate investment has yet to achieve the ultimate goals, you should carefully manage any losses that stem from the property. You should diligently manage your properties in order to optimize and prolong their profits and value.

So, how can you manage your assets?

- Manage any losses and damages
- Manage the consistent flow of income
- Manage your debts
- Lower the interest rate to its lowest
- Pay more than the amount that is assigned

Manage Any Losses and Damages

Everything degrades over time. Real estate is no exception. A leaky roof or wooden beams weakened by termites can eventually damage the house over time if no proper management is taken.

An investor friend of ours who had experienced a lifelong lesson of neglecting his real estate told his story as follows:

In 1993, he bought a modern and beautiful fourplex in the Bay Area. When he was inspecting for termites, there seemed to be no serious problems with it at all. After the purchase of the fourplex, he made minor repairs to the house and started to rent it out. After a short period of time, a family in one of the fourplex units notified him of a leaky roof, which caused water to soak into the walls, and they said they smelled mold. Due to this issue, the family demanded a reduction in their rent.

However, our friend assumed that the family was just making excuses to avoid paying rent or to purposefully try to lower the rent. Thus, he disagreed to reduce the rent. Unfortunately, after a day of heavy rain, a big hole in the roof had flooded the fourplex. As people came to fix the damaged roof and examine the mold in the house, they found out that almost all the sheetrock inside had been plagued with mold. Even though the house looked perfectly normal from the outside, the inside was badly molded to the point where all the surrounding sheetrock of the walls had turned green. At this point, the renter sued him, and he lost a great deal of the suit.

Even if you are able to purchase a property at a low price, if you do not carefully manage your property, you can easily lose money in the process. You should inspect your real estate at least once a year. You should examine to see if there are any termites or damages to the property and, if you should discover any issues, you should find ways to fix them immediately. This method can save you a lump sum of money, as you can avoid encountering serious damages.

Consistently Manage Your Flow of Income

As a long-term investor that uses interest money stemming from the rent to pay for the original debt, it is crucial that you manage your flow of income so that your investment money can generate a consistent flow of profit.

For example, imagine you buy a house for $300K, every month you need to pay the bank $1500 for the interest. In addition to the monthly utilities, tax, and other miscellaneous fees, the total amount that you will need to pay is $1800. If for some reason your real estate is unable to be rented out or you are unable to operate for several months, *the amount that needs to be paid to the bank, along with other essential fees, will have to come out of your own pocket.* Therefore, your investment money and all the efforts that you have poured into that investment do not generate any profits, and you will be on the losing end.

The ability to diligently manage your flow of income such as renting the property out is necessary when applying these long-term strategies. In order for your tenants to continue renting your property in the long run, you should always keep it clean and in good condition to ensure that they have a comfortable living space. Moreover, you should be proactive in decreasing the rent when the economy is at its low point or when the tenants are seriously ill or lose their jobs, in order to help them out during those difficult times.

Tenants usually do not want to move to a different location unless their current location is unsuitable to their needs or in very poor condition, or the rent is unreasonably high. Therefore, just slightly reducing the rent for a short period of time can help in retaining the current tenants, and you won't have to deal with replacing them with new tenants. This can help you significantly because, once the old tenants move out and leave the property for future tenants, *you will need to repaint the house, replace the carpet, or other miscellaneous items. These maintenances and repairs can add up and be quite costly,* and on top of that there will be a waiting period to find new tenants to occupy the property.

A second key to this method is to always have a list of property managers. These people always have a list of potential tenants who are looking to rent a house. You should contact the property managers in your area, or have access to their addresses and phone numbers. If for any reason you need new tenants for your real estate, you will have their contact info handy and a list of interested tenants so you do not have to wait long before renting out your property. Another method is to post advertisements in your local newspaper seeking new tenants before your existing tenants move out.

Manage Your Debt

Reduce the Interest Rate of Loans to its Minimum

"If you just put down 1% interest rate on a home loan and pay a little extra each month, you can save from 20% to 30% of the money you will have to pay the bank and cut short the time to needed to pay the debt by many years."

Professional investors given advice such as instead of cutting coupons to save a few dollars per month, you should seek places that have low interest rates for your mortgage in order to lessen the amount of interest that you have pay to your lender. A few minor changes like this can shorten the repayment period and will also save you a few hundred thousand, or even millions of dollars on property for large and long-term loans.

In the winter of 2006, when Haris first heard of this concept, he felt very excited, and decided to made a phone call to a loan officer who that he had known for many years to learn about it. He also refinanced his house because the interest rate at that time was down at only 3.75%.

After sitting down with the loan officer, he asked for a comparison of numbers. He wanted to know if the amount of interest he was paying was 5.75% / year, and if the interest was lowered to 3.75%, how much could he save?

After a few minutes, the banker showed him the numbers on the computer.

The amount of Haris's mortgage was $ 500,000 dollars, and the interest was 5.75% / year, so each month he was paying the bank $ 2,917.86, and the total amount Haris would pay after 30 years would be $ 1,050,417.23 dollars.

However, with the same $ 500,000 loan with an interest rate of 3.75%, the monthly payment would only be $ 2,315.58, and the total amount paid to the bank after 30 years would only be $833,600.85. By lowering the interest by only 2%, Haris saved $ 216.816.32 USD.

He was elated because such a small change made such a huge difference and saved him a hundreds of thousands of dollars. Haris asked the bank again to help calculate a new figure. If each month he paid an extra $200 dollars toward the mortgage at the 3.75% interest rate, instead of paying $2,315.58 every month, bringing the payment to $2,513.58 monthly, how much more would he benefit?

The banker put the numbers into the computer and just a minute later figured out for Haris that if he paid an extra $200 monthly, the total debt he would pay would only be $ 782,507.49. Additionally, instead of taking 30 years to pay back the loan, if he paid an extra $200 per month, the time to pay off the debt would be reduced by 4 years, meaning his loan would be completely paid off in only 26 years.

Why? This is simply because if you pay an extra amount monthly, it will directly reduce your original debt rather than be put toward paying interest to the bank. That is the secret that the bankers do not want you to know. You can learn more about the numbers and calculating different monthly rates by going to this website:

http://www.mortgagecalculator.org/calculators/what-if-i-pay-more-calculator.php

Or we can look together at the following summary below to see how much money and time you can save if you pay just a little extra a month.

TOTAL AMOUNT AND TIME FRAME OF REPAYMENT TO THE BANK

Loan	Interest Rate	Profits/ Month	Additional Amount of Money Paid/Month	Total Amount Paid to the Bank	Time Frame to Repay Debt
$500,000	3.75 %	$2,315.58	$0	$833,608.06	30 Years
$500,000	3.75 %	$2,315.58	$100	$805,813.29	27 Years and 8 Months
$500,000	3.75 %	$2,315.58	$200	$782,507.49	26 Years and 0 Months
$500,000	3.75 %	$2,315.58	$500	$730,545.77	21 Years and 6 Months
$500,000	3.75 %	$2,315.58	$1000	$677,178.92	17 Years and 8 Months

Attract Good Fortune 7
REPEAT OR EXPAND YOUR SUCCESSES

Reinvesting the profits that you have obtained from prior successes in order to expand even further is very essential when you start out practically empty-handed or with very little capital. If you want to be a millionaire, then you should not lavishly spend the money accumulated from previous investment successes on family vacations, expensive trips, etc. Small investors are satisfied with their small investments in real estate, which prompts them to use the garnered profits on expensive vacations since they do not need to use this money for anything

191

else. However, you are ambitious and you want to become a big time investor in the near future. You realize the fact that wisely managing your money for more investments can expand your wealth for even more luxurious items in life. Starting from now on, you need to live for the future, not just for the present. Successful investors know the importance of reinvesting the profits they acquire in order to expand their earning power. This is something that you should also do. If you do not need to use the profits obtained from the previous investment for daily usage, then you should reinvest that amount.

Using the profits from previous successful investments to reinvest will elevate you to the next step quickly and easily.

After John had sold his first house, instead of thinking about trading in the old Toyota that he bought when he first came to the U.S. for a Lexus, he decided on a different approach. With the profits of $55,000 from the success of that first investment, John could have easily traded his old car for a new one, but he also realized that he could buy two more houses to invest in, which could undoubtedly bring him even more profits. He could have a steady income from renting out the properties, and the possibility of increasing his profits when he sold them.

As for the final decision, John was leaning more towards buying the houses, which was a very wise choice. That was the first step in expanding his real estate investment, which now consists of 300 units. Now, John can even afford to buy a Ferrari worth $220,000, and he does not have to think twice about the cost.

Reinvesting profits from previous successes can:

- Allow you to expand quickly
- Reduce tax
- Give your investment a sense of security
- Greatly increase your assets

REPEAT YOUR SUCCESS AND INCREASE YOUR WEALTH BY USING THE EXCHANGE SYSTEM 1031

Never sell real estate without the advantage of the 1031 Exchange to defer tax payments, because it not only saves you money but also, through it, you can buy other assets if desired.

That is the most useful advice given to me by real estate professionals that helped us in the growth and development of our real estate career.

You can see how by considering that if a real estate investment was earning $300,000 dollars, you would have to pay $100,000 or $150,000 dollars in taxes, but if you defer taxes by using the 1031 exchange, you could use the $300,000 for continued investments. Then, the subsequent real estate investment would maybe earn US $ 200,000 more, then you can continue to defer taxes and have $500,000 that you can use to invest further.

You can go on this way continuing to defer taxes until you want to stop investing.

Could this happen in America, where there are very strict tax laws? The answer is yes. It is through an IRS program called the 1031 exchange.

So what is the 1031 exchange?

The 1031 exchange is a program from the IRS that allow taxpayers to use the accumulated profits earned from the sale of an old investment property for new investment properties so that they do not have to pay taxes on profits until much later.

This is a huge advantage of owning real estate over owning stocks and bonds because there is no similar convention for stocks and bonds. Additionally, with the 1031 program, you can control the amount of money in the transaction process.

This program is very useful. However, to be eligible for tax-deferment, you need to have the expertise of a tax guide, or you must understand the requirements of the IRS. Or, you can learn from the experience from a real estate tax expert. Even in extremely difficult cases, however, you can understand how to succeed in delaying taxes by following the six principles below.

1. Keep Your Real Estate At Least One Year and One Day

Regardless of whether it is an old or a new property that you are trying to sell, you should hold on to any properties that you have. Any property has its own value when it comes to an investment. According to tax regulations, you have to keep your property for *at least a year and several days.*

2. Limit the Amount of Properties to Three or Fewer

Starting from the day that you sell your property, you have 45 days to submit a list of properties that you want to purchase. In that list, you should have three houses or fewer. It expires after 45 days, and you cannot extend it any longer.

Limiting yourself to three or fewer properties can actually help you from making mistakes. In addition, the price of three properties cannot exceed twice the amount of the property that you just sold. For example, you sold your old property for $100,000, and you immediately search for three more properties to buy. If each property is worth $30,000, the total will be $90,000. If each one is worth $50,000, it will total up to $150,000 for all three properties.

So why is it three properties and not just one? Why not less than three or more than three, like four or five? The answer to this question is to avoid landing in a situation where, if you only list one property and it happens to not sell, you may not have enough time to secure another property to replace that one and after the 45 days required by the IRS. You will no longer be eligible for that program. In contrast, if you list more than four properties, then there will be a lot more management that needs to be done. You can also land in a situation where the total of the four or five properties added together exceeds twice the amount of the property that you just sold. This type of exchange is not very successful.

Therefore, learning from past experience, you should *simplify your list to just three properties or fewer.*

3. Have a Full Understanding of the Strong Points of Each House or Property

If the IRS wants to inspect your work, their staff can come straight to you to confirm the filings. Therefore, you want to make sure your list is up to date with all the street address, number of rooms, and bathrooms that each house has. You should also carefully describe the empty lots that do not have an address. You will *need to send the information to the IRS before midnight of the 45th day.* You can send it directly to the IRS, or through email, or fax, as long as all the information is turned in promptly. After midnight of the 45th day, you can no longer alter your listing. If the IRS finds out that you have altered any information after the deadline, you will be punished severely and might even be sent to jail.

4. Complete the Purchase and Sale of Property Within 180 Days

Starting from the day you complete the sale of the old property, you have 180 days to purchase a new property (this new property has to be on the list that was sent to the IRS). You can buy one or all three properties on that list, as required within 45 days. *The 45-day timeframe refers to when the list has to be sent in to the IRS, whereas the 180-day period indicates the timeframe in which the purchase or sale of a property has to be completed.* These time frames cannot be extended.

5. Confirm That the Old and New Owner of the Property Is the Same

The name of the owner that is listed for the old property should correspond with name of the owner on the new property. For example, if "A and B" sells their luxurious mansion, then the name "A and B" should also be on the list for the new ownership. They cannot change it to "AB" or "A" or "B".

6. Buy Something Else of the Same or Higher Value

In order to avoid paying taxes during the exchange process, you need to purchase a property that is either equal or higher in value than the previous property. In addition, you should reinvest any profits that you might have garnered. For instance, if A and B sell a property with a price of $100,000, they will need to purchase a new property with a price of at least $100,000. If they only pay $90,000 for their new property, then they would need to pay the remaining $10,000 in tax.

There is no limit to the number of exchanges you can do. You can continuously obtain the profits from selling an old property in exchange for a new property until you decide to take a portion of the interest from the sale of those properties. When that happens, you will need to pay taxes. Through this method, you can actually manage your income, which will potentially be taxed during the process of reinvesting. The exchange process allows you to simultaneously utilize your cash flow without having to worry about paying taxes.

Attract Good Fortune 8
MAKE YOUR DEVELOPMENT EVEN STRONGER

In order to become a large-scale investor, relying on your own money is simply not enough. You need to know how to utilize your capital as leverage for greater financial gains; then your capital will exponentially increase. Each of your successes will increase your capital and you can accumulate those for an even greater amount of capital for the next investment. This process is similar to a snowball; the more you earn, the greater amount of capital you will garner from the outside. The more capital you can obtain from the outside, the more active you will be in this field. If you go big on your investments such as through joint-ventures with other investors, you will garner more money in return, which will exponentially increase your capital.

THAT SPECTACULAR DAY WILL COME SOONER THAN YOU THINK

Once your system of investment has solidified, you will be ready to take the next big step. This step signifies the fact that you are ready to repeatedly expand your branch of investment in many other places.

You should remember the fact that even a small success in investment can trigger a career in real estate investment. When your system of investment is in place, you can readily participate in the world of investment. This means that you can now repeatedly expand your investment to not only the area of your residence, but also anywhere in the U.S. and even other parts of the world.

Throughout this book, we have gone through a quite a journey. We started out with a dream of becoming wealthy through real estate investments, and we have actually learned the methods to making that dream a reality. We have formulated an investment plan to expand it into a million dollar business. And now, we will discuss how your career can garner even more assets.

The first point that needs to be addressed is that, when you start an investment, you need to have an idea of which direction it is heading. This means that one day, you will want your name to be amongst those of other millionaires. You need to be clear of the potential opportunities and strengthen your business as you deem appropriate. Now, you need to realize two important paths in real estate investment in order to obtain millions of dollars.

- First, you need to develop a system of investment that has been successful before.
- Second, utilize the financial value of that system as leverage in order to obtain a great amount of interest that is even more than the amount of money you currently have.
- Repeatedly write down your goals, formulate a detailed action plan, and review your plan every day. Pour all of your efforts into becoming an excellent investor in the field you have chosen. You can always go the extra mile and

accomplish your dreams of becoming a wealthy investor through dedication, motivation, and sacrifice. That task is not too difficult as it just needs a bit of diligence and hard work in the early stages. You will be able to reap many great benefits in the near future.

EPILOGUE

Nothing in life can replace the ability to endure. You strive every day to achieve your ultimate goals. In the end, you will become the most important figure in your local community. You will have everything that you had hoped for, and you will always be in possession of a loaded bank account. Moreover, you will feel satisfied and proud of your achievements, knowing that you have achieved everything you have planned and hoped for. All these positive attributes depend on you to strive further in your career and to never give up. You can achieve it all.

Becoming a millionaire from real estate investment is a lot quicker than you might have initially thought.

Even just a small success in your initial investment is enough to be a stepping stone for you to achieve your ultimate goals. Always be patient in finding the path to success. The knowledge presented in this book includes various negative experiences from real estate investors. You are more fortunate than those millionaires because you have access to their experiences and life lessons to guide you through this journey. Gradually, the process of becoming a millionaire will happen sooner than you think.

The plans and skills that we have mentioned above, especially the newer skills, may seem complicated to you at the moment. However, you should always remember to ask for more information each step of the way. Once you have completed every step, the path will become much smoother. In order to succeed in investment, you should have a good understanding of the necessary skills. Success in investment is not solely based on your luck. However, success stems from knowledge and skills, and the application of both. Nowadays, anyone can succeed in investment, regardless of where your starting point is, or whether you have the appropriate knowledge or experience in the field. Every essential skill needed to succeed can be learned along the way. Whatever other people can achieve, you can too!

www.ingramcontent.com/pod-product-compliance
Lightning Source LLC
Chambersburg PA
CBHW070358200326
41518CB00011B/1972

* 9 7 8 1 9 2 8 1 5 5 6 7 6 *